Walking in Weardale

By

Keven Shevels

First published in Great Britain in 2012 by Trailguides Limited.
www.trailguides.co.uk

ISBN 978-1-905444-53-3

The route diagrams in this book are based upon 1925-1940 Ordnance Survey One-Inch maps updated by field trips and site visits.

Trailguides Limited
35 Carmel Road South
Darlington
Co Durham DL3 8DQ

Cover design by Steve Gustard
Artwork by Trailguides Limited

CONTENTS

Cover photos.
Front cover. Crossing Fine Burn. Walk 6. Pawlaw Pike.
Back cover. The upper reaches of the Killhope Burn. Walk 8. Cowhorse Hush & Cuthbert's Level.

INTRODUCTION

1. Introduction

Taking it's name from the river which starts with the joining of several small streams at Wearhead, the dale stretches from the high moors above Killhope to the flatter, lower lands just east of Wolsingham. The scenery changes as the river travels down the dale, from the bleak, heather clad moors and rocky outcrops to gently undulating stone walled fields. The river itself changing too, from a small rocky rushing flow of water it gradually absorbs tributaries on it's descent through the dale to become wider and slower as it becomes, ultimately, one of the great rivers of the North of England.

Weardale is basically a farming area, although for centuries the wealth of it's minerals and underlying stone have created industries that in the past have created both riches and poverty for it's inhabitants. One of the lead dales of the North Pennines, which made Britain the centre of the world's lead industry during the 18th and 19th centuries, lead was only one of the underground treasures which kept the extraction industries going well into the 20th century when they finally met their demise.

Today the population of the dale is much smaller than it was two hundred years ago and, aside from agriculture which is still a vital part of the dale's economy, much of the dale is benefiting from an increasing growth in tourism. In particular, the walker can experience here a full and varied landscape from the fields and meadows of the lower dale, the purple clad heather grouse moors in summer and, at the top end of the dale, one of the wildest and bleakest unspoilt natural landscapes in Britain.

Weardale is very much an under appreciated and relatively undiscovered part of Britain and for the walker, who can really understand what this valley can offer, then long may it be so.

2. Access & the Right to Roam

In the heyday of the lead industry, the miners of Weardale were considered to have the right to walk along any route they choose unimpeded by the landowner particularly if this was on the way to or from the mine. Over time this 'freedom' led to the development of many of the footpaths that exist today.

Nowadays, we have a mixture of access rights within the dale with access in the lower farmed areas being legally restricted only to public rights of way such as footpaths and bridleways. This is reflected in those routes within this book that cross the lower part of the valley.

With the implementation of the Countryside Right of Way Act 2000 in 2005 and the introduction of the "Right to Roam" this has changed some of the access rights and certain upland areas of Weardale have now become legally accessible away from public rights of way. This legislation allows walkers the right to roam at will over "designated access land" without the need to be restricted to official footpaths and bridleways.

On the new editions of the Ordnance Survey Explorer maps, this new access land is marked with a light yellow coloured background and at the entry points to this land, the stiles and gates carry the new "access land" waymarking symbol of a brown stick man in a brown circle.

The details that accompany each of the walk descriptions will provide information as to whether the route uses rights of way or crosses open access land.

With the right to access has also come responsibility and the walker is expected to observe various limits and restrictions that are placed on their activities at certain times of the year. The landowner and/or farmer has the right to exclude access for up to twenty eight days per year and this is normally applied between May and early July to coincide with the breeding season of the ground-nesting birds on the moors. Where they are known, restrictions that may impinge on any given walk are shown in the details for that walk. However, don't take it for granted that these are going to be accurate as in each year these restrictions may change. Always check any notices that are placed at the access points for any restrictions. To find out more about out the `right to roam` and whether any general or specific restrictions apply to any part of Weardale then a visit to the website **www.countrysideaccess.gov.uk** will give you all the necessary information.

With using the right to roam and moving away from the recognised footpaths and bridleways, the walker does become more exposed to potential hazards. As with most parts of the North Pennines, Weardale has been heavily exploited for its mineral wealth and this can be clearly seen in the number of old mines and quarries that are visible from these walks. This has left a legacy of old workings, quarries and shafts, all of which can be hazardous. Caution must always be exercised when in the vicinity of any of these sites.

3. The Walks

The nine walks in this book have all been designed to explore the woods, hills and moors while showcasing the landscape and history of this dale. The walks start from a number of different locations and the map opposite will give you a guide to these positions.

Anybody who has used one of my books before will realise that I have a little bit of a passion for history and how this is reflected in the landscape. As always this is shown within these walks as I quite frequently use them to visit and explore certain aspects of the countryside that I, personally, find quite interesting. I don't believe that walking guidebooks should be boring and, hopefully, the walks and associated notes will help convey my enthusiasm for the valley of Weardale to you, both as a reader and as a walker.

In the details preceding each of the walks there is an approximate time taken for that particular walk which includes a reasonable time to explore the various sites of interest that are visited. However, this can be variable depending upon how long you, as the walker, take to explore these sites. If you chose not to have a look and investigate then the time taken will obviously be shorter whereas if you linger and have a good mooch about then you may be longer than I have estimated.

With the huge impact that lead mining had on the dale, it is perhaps inevitable that a number of these walks pass old lead mines and workings and with some of the routes these are actually a feature of the walk. However, resist any temptation to enter and explore these openings as it is extremely dangerous to do so. It is over one hundred years since some of these mines were abandoned and during the intervening period there has been no maintenance work carried out in them with the result that both rot and erosion has taken it's toll and many of these levels are no longer stable.

The walks in this book have all been graded in accordance with the Ferguson Grading System ('FGS') and the actual grading is set out at the beginning of each individual walk to help you assess their difficulty. A detailed explanation of the FGS and how individual gradings are determined is set out on pages 107-109 in the Appendix to this book.

4. The Weather

Weardale forms part of the North Pennines and, as with most of this range of hills, the weather here can be very changeable even during summer. The top end of the dale reaches some of the highest hills in County Durham and the exposed altitude of this part of the county can make even a balmy summer's day seem cold and uninviting. When you are near the top of one of these high hills, mist and low cloud can be experienced at any time of the year and can roll in quite quickly catching the walker unaware.

Don't misjudge this high country, when walking at any time of the year be prepared and equipped for all weather conditions. Even in summer it is always ad-

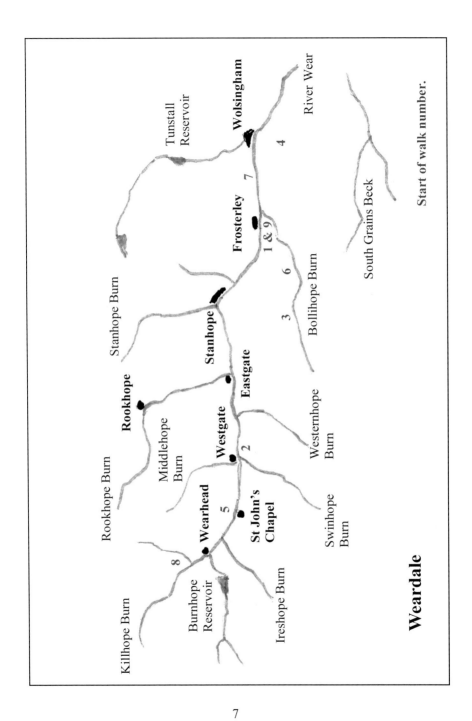

Weardale

Tunstall Reservoir

Wolsingham

River Wear

Stanhope Burn

7

Frosterley

1 & 9

4

Stanhope

6

3

Bollihope Burn

South Grains Beck

Rookhope

Eastgate

Rookhope Burn

Middlehope Burn

Westgate

2

Westernhope Burn

Killhope Burn

Wearhead

5

St John's Chapel

Swinhope Burn

8

Burnhope Reservoir

Ireshope Burn

Start of walk number.

7

visable to carry a waterproof and some form of warm clothing. Despite global warming there is still a strong prospect of snow during the winter months and whereas the majority of the paths and tracks are easily followed during most of the year, if there is a layer of snow this can make some of them extremely difficult to follow.

5. The Maps

Unfortunately Weardale is one of those unlucky locations that falls on several different maps. The bulk of the dale is shown on OL31 The North Pennines, Teesdale and Weardale, with part of the north side of the valley being shown on OL307 Consett and Derwent Reservoir. The small area of land to the east of Wolsingham that is generally considered to be part of the dale is covered by the map OL305 Bishop Auckland.

As far as possible, I've tried to keep the walks in this book confined to the one map so that you don't have to carry two maps with you. But the best of intentions does not always work out and you may, on occasions, have to carry more than one map.

The relevant map will be shown in the details of the individual walk.

The route descriptions included in this book are meant as a guide and although under normal conditions they should be sufficient to guide you round the route they are not intended to replace the use of the relevant map. This countryside can be wild and rough, which is part of it's attraction, and at the same time the weather can be very changeable. It is very possible to set off in brilliant sunshine and then to find that later, low cloud and rain has come rolling in and visibility is very poor. The ability to navigate with map and compass is a required skill to safely traverse these hills and it would be extremely foolhardy to venture out with just this guidebook and no map.

6. Tourist Information Centres & Websites

There is just the one visitor centre in the whole of Weardale which is based in Stanhope at the Durham Dales Centre.

Durham Dales Centre, Castle Gardens, Stanhope, Weardale, Co Durham. DL13 2FJ

Telephone 01388 527650.

The centre is open 7 days a week, but times vary through the year dependent upon season.

At the time of writing (2012), due to budgetary constraints, discussions are being held over the future of the TIC and replacing it with an on-line service. Hopefully nothing will come of these proposals and the Centre will continue for many years into the future.

In addition to the TIC, the Dales Centre hosts other facilities such as tea room, craft shops and conference facilities.

The majority of Weardale lies within the North Pennines Area of Outstanding Natural Beauty. Although the AONB does not operate any visitor centres in Weardale they do organise activities throughout the North Pennines, including this dale, and have a very useful website giving information on flora, fauna, geology, attractions and events in the North Pennines. The website can be found at **www.northpennines.org.uk**

7. Mining and Quarrying

Lead and iron mining have been important to the economy of the dale since early times. It is not known when mining actually started in the dale but the earliest reference dates back to 1154 when King Stephen granted his nephew, the then Bishop of Durham, Hugh Piuset, the additional mineral rights to extract silver from the lead already being mined in Weardale. This importance and dependence on mining resulted in a greater population density than would normally be expected from such a high and fairly remote valley.

After the Norman Conquest, the dale was given into the ownership of the Bishop of Durham and as landowner he was able to grant mining leases for exploration and exploitation of the dale's mineral riches, in return receiving one-tenth of all ore produced or it's monetary value. The mines provided an extremely large part of the income for the Bishop's estate but this also applied to the vicar of Stanhope as well. As the clergyman responsible for the large parish of Stanhope, which covered all of the upper dale, he received a tithe or tenth of all output of the dale to support both him and the church. This made the vicar one of the richest clergymen in the country and the position was one of the most sought after in the church establishment.

The needs of mining and quarrying encouraged improvements in communication and transport in the dale with the valley eventually having two separate railway systems running into it. As lead mining declined in the late 1800's, the mining of iron ore and fluorspar grew in importance and while mining in other parts of the North Pennines withered away, these two minerals ensured that the industry continued in Weardale into the middle and later parts of the 20th century.

The growth of the iron industry during the 19th century and it's need for limestone to use as a flux during the smelting process, led to the opening of large quarries for it's extraction. These now form a very prominent feature along both sides of the valley between Frosterley and Stanhope.

Also required by the iron industry was ganister, a form of sandstone with a high silica content, which was used for lining the furnaces. The fells south of St John's Chapel were the source for this and the waste heaps from the quarries form a prominent feature on the skyline.

The effects of lead mining on the landscape are more visible on the upper fells, where hushes, spoil heaps and shafts mark the line of many of the veins. Ruins and artefacts from the early days of the industry are, unfortunately, not quite so numerous as in other dales but with careful observation can be found and can tell a fascinating story. The mines that were still in use into the 20th century have been closed and, in the main, made inaccessible.

8. Lead Mining Glossary

A few of the terms used in the text of the book may be unfamiliar to those not used to the lead mining industry and so a brief glossary is listed below to help you better understand some of the features that you will encounter on the walks.

Dressing floor

An area where the lead ore would be crushed and processed to remove the waste prior to going to the smelt mill. During this process, or dressing as it was known, the ore would be crushed and ground up until it was the consistency of sand with the final product produced from this process being know as lead concentrate. The dressing floor would usually be close to the mine entrance so that there would be no costly transporting of waste material, only the valuable lead concentrate would be moved to the smelt mill.

Hush

A rather environmentally unfriendly method of extracting ore from the ground. A dam would be erected at the top of a slope and a head of water built up, this would then be released in a torrent to flow down the slope scouring off the top soil and other loose rock exposing the vein of lead, the vein would then be worked with hammer and pick. Hushes were often used in the exploratory stage to determine both where the vein was and in which direction it ran. In most cases the hush didn't tend to go deep into the vein and so they were then often followed by driving a level at the bottom of the hush to access the lower levels of ore.

Flue

The chimney from a smelt mill. They often ran a considerable distance up the side of a hill before terminating in a chimney on the hill top. Built to remove the toxic fumes from the smelting process, they also provided a secondary purpose in creating a draught for the furnaces helping to increase their operating temperature.

Leat

A man-made water channel built to carry a flow of water to a specific location.

Level

A horizontal tunnel dug into the side of the hill to access the vein, a level was also known as an adit. Normally located at the bottom of the hill they would usually be constructed with a slight upward angle to allow water from the mine to drain out. Drainage was a secondary purpose of a level and is why many of them have a small stream running out of them. Nowadays the entrances of many of them are quite often silted up due to this water flow. In most cases, levels and shafts connect underground to form a complex of tunnels.

Shaft

A vertical tunnel dug straight down into the vein. Normally located on the top of a hill, shafts are distinguished by a round ring or "donut" of spoil that circled the opening of the shaft. Shafts could be deep or shallow with the deeper ones often connecting to levels. Shallower shafts would only be around 30 metres deep with a number of them forming a straight line across the moor as they follow the line of the vein. Shallow shafts are also known as bell pits.

Smelt mill

A building where the lead was extracted by heating the lead concentrate in a furnace until the molten lead would separate from the rock.

Spoil

The waste material from the mining process that is discarded around the mine and processing sites. Nowadays all waste is just generally called spoil although during the days of mining there were specific names for waste from different parts of the process such as "deads" for non-ore bearing rock and stone extracted from the mine.

Looking across to the windmills above Tow Law.

WALK 1: FATHERLEY HILL & WOLSINGHAM PARK MOOR

A medium distance walk that crosses the low moors to the north of Frosterley and which has links to the prehistoric past. The hills here are low lying compared to the ones further up the dale and flow down to join the plains of Mid-Durham. Although not of great height, they still present opportunities for excellent walking and some outstanding views over the lower lying lands to the east. The majority of this walk is over open access land and so is not that often walked, take the opportunity for some quiet reflection.

DISTANCE: 9.5 mile / 15.2 km.
ASCENT: 1,512 feet / 461 metres.
TERRAIN: A long steady climb up a tarmac track leads onto the open moor where moorland tracks and paths are followed. These moorland tracks and paths are, in the most part, well defined and easily followed although there is an optional stretch of 300 metres that is pathless and involves heather bashing. Not all of these tracks have a hard surface and during the winter months and after bad weather may be wet and muddy.
START: Frosterley Station car park. GR. NZ 024 369.
MAP: The bulk of this walk is on map OL307 Consett & Derwent Reservoir, however, the initial stages up the tarmac lane to the open moor are on OL31 North Pennines.
DOGS: Not allowed on the access land.
ACCESS: This route uses some public rights of way but in the main crosses open access land.

GRID REFERENCES

Frosterley Station	024 369
Gate	025 385
Fatherley Hill Currick	023 395
Track/path junction	022 398
Shooting box	038 410
Track junction	040 412
Track	036 423
Collier Law	017 417
Frosterley Station	024 369

FGS GRADING
Grading is F7 [D1, N1, T1, R2, H2]

Distance	1	6 – 12 miles
Navigation	1	Basic navigation skills needed
Terrain	1	50 – 75% on graded track or path 25 – 50% off track
Remoteness	2	Countryside not in close proximity to habitation – less than 20% of the route within 2 miles
Height	2	Over 125 ft per mile

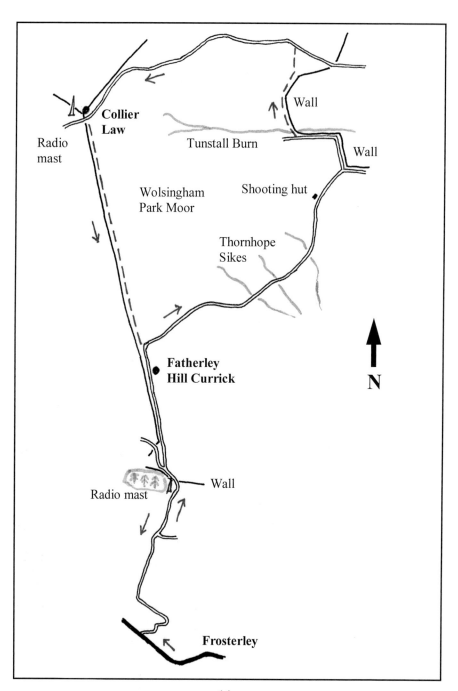

Collier Law

Radio mast

Tunstall Burn

Wall

Wall

Wolsingham Park Moor

Shooting hut

Thornhope Sikes

Fatherley Hill Currick

N

Wall

Radio mast

Frosterley

THE WALK

1. Leave the station car park and turn right to head up to the main road and once there, turn left to head out of the village. About 100 metres after the last house a tarmac track comes down at an acute angle to join the right side of the road. See photo below. Cross the road and follow the track as it climbs quite steeply. This

The tarmac track leaving the main road.

is a long steady climb up the side of the valley and eventually the radio mast at Rogerley High Plantation comes into view. Continue following the track up to the mast and here the track bears left to enter the mast's compound and there is a gate in front leading on to the open moor. **GR 025 385.**

2. Go through the gate and follow the track as it bears to the left to follow the outside of the wall. After a short distance the main track turns to the right and a fainter green track continues straight on and here bear right following the main track. After a short distance a fence line appears on the left, it is hard to tell whether the fence joins the track or the track joins the fence. However, continue along the track and the very distinguishable mound of Fatherley Hill and it's currick, or pile of stones, is soon reached. **GR 023 395.**

Approaching Fatherley Hill Currick.

3. Continue following the track as it runs next to the fence. After a short distance you'll come to a junction where a well-used path continues straight on following the fence line and the track bears to the right away from the fence. **GR 022 398.**

4. Follow the track as it bears right to head across Wolsingham Park Moor. Initially the track runs across the moor before it starts to descend towards the valley and eventually run by the side of a line of grouse butts. After descending next to the butts, the track then bears to the left to run across the side of the hill and, after a short distance, crosses Thornhope Sike and then after a further 250 metres, a second unnamed sike. Just few metres after this sike, on the right hand side of the track lies the disturbed remains of a small burial mound, see photo.

The remains of the burial mound next to the track.

A few metres after the burial mound and also on the right side of the track lies an intricately marked stone. Full of curved lines and depressions, it is easy to visualise this stone as some form of artwork but the markings on it are entirely natural and made by nature not the hand of man.

The marked stone next to the track.

Continue following the track, for quite a while you will have seen a large indistinct shape on the horizon, now as you get closer it is easier to recognise the outline of a building. After a short while, the track does arrive at the side of this small stone building with it's wooden annexe, the building serving as a shooting box or hut. **GR 038 410.**

The lonely shooting hut high up on the moors.

5. Continue following the track and as it starts to bear to the right, you'll come to a junction with another track on the left. **GR 040 412.**

At this point you are at the closest that you are going to get to the big white windmills above Tow Law. Strange how you get used to them and they just become part of the landscape.

6. Turn on to the side track and follow it round the outside of the wall to come, after 350 metres, to a cross wall in front and a gate. Don't go through the gate but instead turn left to follow the quad bike track running along the outside of the wall. Follow this for 400 metres to come to the wall corner where the track continues straight ahead over the open moor but instead of following it, turn right to follow the path that continues running alongside the wall. After a few metres you'll have to cross the infant Tunstall Burn but unless weather conditions are really bad then this is not too much of a problem. Here the Tunstall Burn is still only young and has over 2 km to go and several tributaries to pick up before it enters Tunstall Reservoir.

The infant Tunstall Burn.

Once across the burn, the path next to the wall does get fainter but the walking is not too bad. Keep following the wall and after 300 metres the wall has a slight corner in it and starts to curve to the right. After another 200 metres there is another slight corner and the wall curves again to the right and here you have a route choice. Straight ahead, about 300 metres across the heather beds, lies a track that is coming in to join the wall further along. If you wish, you can cut the corner by going straight across the heather to meet the track, no real problem doing this as the track lies straight in front and even if you go slightly off-course you are still going to meet the track somewhere along it's length. If you do go across the heather then, as you are crossing, the tops of two shooting huts will become visible over on the left and you will reach the track round about **GR 036 423**. The alternative to crossing the heather is to continue following the wall until you come to a wall corner and gate and here the same track joins you.

7. Irrespective of which route you take, turn left on to the track and follow it past the two shooting huts and up the long steady climb to Collier Law and it's radio mast. After just over 2 km of steady walking you arrive at the top of Collier Law and come to a gate in a fence. **GR 017 417.**

The cairn on top of Collier Law.

The actual top of Collier Law is off to the right of the track, a few metres higher and topped with a stone cairn, round which a fence junction has been built. The stone cairn is built on a 'lump' on top of the hill, surprisingly the wooden fence that runs over it's top looks as if it has actually been built over the top of the cairn. Like the mound on Fatherley Hill, the top of Collier Law has the look of a Bronze Age burial mound and also fits the known pattern of these artefacts, a mound located on the top of a prominent hill, highly visible from the surrounding countryside. This one may be marking another boundary of the settlements located on the sides of these hills.

8. Don't go through this gate but instead turn left to follow the path running on the left of the fence and heading to the distant Fatherley Hill. When you get closer, you'll join the track that you followed out across the moor after you visited the hill on the outward journey. Re-join the track now and follow it as it heads back over the shoulder of Fatherley Hill and after that, when you come to the wall in front, bear to the left towards the radio mast where you'll go back through the gate and re-join the tarmac lane. Follow the lane back down the side of the valley to the main road and then turn left to return to Frosterley.

FATHERLEY HILL CURRICK

As you approach Fatherley Hill, the shape of it catches your attention as it has the appearance of a small hill built on top of the moor and is very reminiscent of a Bronze Age burial mound. Although nothing is recorded, this is not beyond possibility. Mounds were built from large quantities of stone quite literally piled on top of each other, although nowadays, after several thousand years of weather and ground changes, many of them have now naturally turfed over. However, mounds of a considerable size do exist in other parts of the county and Kirkcarrion in Teesdale was documented as having sufficient stone to build all the walls of Crossthwaite Pasture.

Looking at it, the top of the hill presents a green, turf-covered mound with a considerable amount of stones poking their way out. There are a number of very large boulders as part of the top of the hill, stones that would have been very difficult for men, with no lifting tools, to move. However, even if these are natural then they could have been incorporated within the structure, with the rest of the mound being built around them.

The top of the hill is named on the OS map as Fatherley Hill Currick. The word currick comes from Cumbric, the ancient tongue of the Celts of northern England and southern Scotland and means 'pile of stones' and may not necessarily refer to the stone cairn on top of the hill but rather to the mound itself. If Bronze Age, then the stones would have been old long before the Celts came.

The square chamber in the side of the mound.

A couple of metres to the north east of the summit cairn lies a small scoop into the hill. Unusually, this has the appearance of a small, square, stone-lined chamber which has been built into the mound and then at some point uncovered. See photo. Such chambers within a mound were not uncommon and they contained either the interred remains or ashes of the deceased. In many parts of the country, folk tales sprang up about these mounds containing treasure troves and during the 1700 and 1800's many were broken into by 'enterprising' locals and antiquarians. This may explain the number of scoops, or possible excavations, around the side of the hill,

Burial mounds on the top of hills do not exist in isolation, they were a factor in the burial service of a prominent and important individual but it is also thought that they existed as territorial markers and status symbols. The statement 'Look this is our land and you can see how wealthy and powerful we are by the way that we bury our dead' still reverberates through the landscape even today. The fact that they didn't occur on their own usually means that not too far away there would have been a settlement and evidence of the remains of round houses has been found further down the slope on the west of Fatherley Hill. Being a predominately agricultural society there may also be evidence of field systems and the related walls hidden away under the heather and peat. The remains of field walls and round houses have been identified on the Stanhope side of Fatherley Hill, that plus the evidence of the Heathery Burn Hoard, one of the richest Bronze Age finds ever made in Britain and found close to the Stanhope Burn, indicates that during this period the area was an extremely rich and prosperous one.

After reading this article and sitting at Fatherley Hill Currick looking out over the open moor, it may seem hard to visualise how such agricultural wealth could materialise. But over time landscapes and weather patterns change and four thousand years ago this moorland did not exist. By the Bronze Age, large expanses of the natural forest that had once covered the landscape of the entire country had been cleared. The valley floors and the sides of the hills that we would now cultivate were then subject to flooding, were often water-logged and were heavily overgrown. Settlements and farmland were higher up the hill than where they would be nowadays and here the wooded areas of birch, oak and elm were cleared to produce rich, flowing grassland where cattle ranching was the primary agricultural activity. Movement of people, livestock and goods was also done across these higher levels and whereas these burial mounds can not be seen from where we now travel along the valley floors, they would have been easily visible and distinctive to a population moving across these hills.

The trig point and observation tower on Windy Hill.
Walk 2. The Mineral Line & Windy Hill.

WALK 2: THE MINERAL LINE & WINDY HILL

A walk of two distinctive halves. The first part of the walk follows the route of an old mineral railway opened up in the 1800's, as it gently curves it's way round the side of the dale to the terminus in the Rookhope valley. The second half is true fell walking over wide, open moor to attain the summit of the rarely visited, at least by walkers, Windy Hill.

DISTANCE: 8.9 mile / 14.2 km
ASCENT: 1,247 feet / 380 metres
TERRAIN: After an initial steep climb up the road out of Westgate, the route following the old mineral line over to Rookhope is relatively gentle and unde-manding although there is a steep descent down to the crossing of the Park Burn due to the railway embankment over the burn having disappeared. In places where the line goes through a cutting, the ground within the cutting may be a bit wet and boggy and it may be better to walk to one side along the top of the bank. The return from Rookhope is a long steady climb over fairly pathless moor to the summit trig on Windy Hill before descending back down to West-gate, part of which involves a lengthy road section.
TIME: 5 hours.
START: Large lay-by on the north side of the road, opposite the caravan site, as you pass through Westgate. GR NY 906 380.
MAP: OL307 Consett and Derwent Reservoir.
DOGS: Even though dogs are allowed on the public rights of way and there does not appear to be any restrictions on them over the access land this may not be a suitable route to take your dog. There are quite a number of fences and gates where they will need to be lifted over plus there is the proximity of the open shaft at Park Burn and although there is both a small distance and a wire fence between you and the steep drops into Heights Quarry they are still there.
ACCESS: The route is all on public rights of way apart from the stretch used to access the summit trig point on Windy Hill where you cross open access land.

GRID REFERENCES

Lay-by	906 380
Road/track junction	910 387
Park Burn	921 388
Track after Heights Quarry	930 390
Track junction	937 428
Wall corner	935 424

Windy Hill	917 413
Roadside	912 405
Lay-by	906 380

FGS GRADING

Grading is F7 [D1, N1, T2, R1, H2]

Distance	1	6 – 12 miles
Navigation	1	Basic navigation skills needed
Terrain	2	25 -50% on graded track or path 50 – 75% off track
Remoteness	1	Countryside in fairly close proximity to habitation – at least 80% of the route within 2 miles
Height	2	Over 125 ft per mile

The old track bed of the Weardale Iron Company Railway.

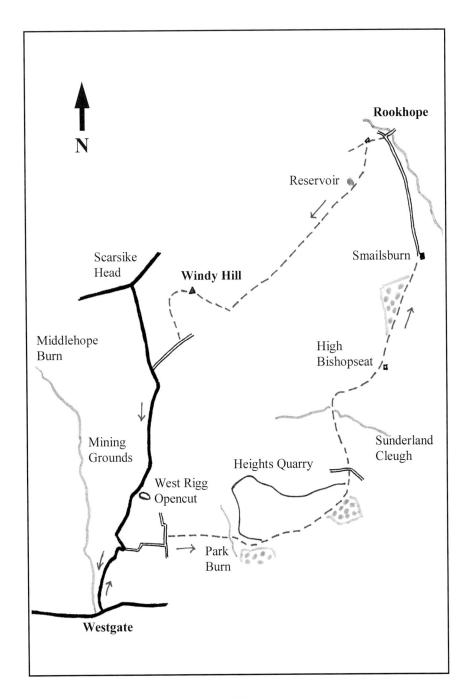

N

Rookhope

Reservoir

Scarsike
Head

Windy Hill

Smailsburn

Middlehope
Burn

High
Bishopseat

Mining
Grounds

Heights Quarry

Sunderland
Cleugh

West Rigg
Opencut

Park
Burn

Westgate

THE WALK.

1. From the lay-by follow the valley floor road through Westgate towards Stanhope and after passing the village Co-Op store, turn left up the side road signposted to Rookhope. At the time of test walking this route, the sign to Rookhope had been twisted slightly and so wasn't pointing directly up the side road. Follow the road as it heads uphill out of the village. After passing Spot House on the left, the road starts to climb quite steeply as it goes up Peat Hill and there is a bit of a gap before you encounter the next house on the left. Just after this building the road does a sharp left hand bend and here, on the right hand side of the road, is a tarmac lane with two public footpath signposts. **GR 910 387.**

The lane leaving the road.

2. Turn right to leave the road and follow the tarmac lane, ignoring the path that goes down the track to Dalehead Farm Cottages. Go past the two houses on the left where the tarmac ends and the lane becomes a track. Just after this the lane turns left before turning right again. At this corner you can see through an open gateway in front, the slightly raised embankment of the old mineral railway which you will soon join. Continue on the track and after a short distance you'll come to a gate across the lane with a waymarker on the right hand side and a small kissing gate on the left of the main gate. Go through the kissing gate and you'll find that the wall on the left hand side of the lane has now disappeared but you'll soon come to a waymarked junction. Here turn left for a few metres to come to a waymarked gate and stile on the right side. At this point you will be joining the route of the old mineral railway and even if now the old track bed is no more than a grass track, it is still easy to determine and see where it passes across the field and through the gate.

Before you turn right to go through the gate look straight ahead up the track to see the remains of a double lime kiln just a couple of hundred metres in front. Easy enough to visit before coming back to the gate.

The old lime kiln.

Either cross the stile or go through the gateway onto the old rail line and follow it. As you may have guessed, the old line is easy to follow and presents no real navigation difficulties although there are a few gates and stiles to cross.

The gate and stile leading onto the old railway.

After a few hundred metres you'll come to a small stone wall on the left side of the track and a couple of metres after that a large concrete base with large metal bolts sticking out of it that obviously used to secure some form of fixture, possibly a derrick or small crane. This was the top of the Scutter Hill Incline where wagons were hauled up from the valley floor by stationary engine to join the

Passing the top of the Scutter Hill Incline and, inset, the concrete block.

main line. Continue to follow the track bed and after a while you'll approach a belt of trees on the left side of the rail line. When you cross the fence in front of them you'll see that the track bed continues on a high embankment to cross the Park Burn. Or at least it once did, either as a result of floods or erosion the middle section of the embankment has now disappeared leaving an uncrossable gap, which is quite probably the reason why the Weardale Way, which once used this route, was rerouted. Feel free to go and have a look at the missing gap if you wish but afterwards you'll still need to come back to the stile that you have just crossed. From the stile you'll need to turn left down the north side of the embankment to follow a path that runs down the edge of the bank through the trees. This brings you down onto the floor next to the burn. **GR 921 388.**

Caution– the path brings you down next to a large boulder alongside a small fenced enclosure. The enclosure houses an old, open shaft, an air shaft linking into mine workings below. Peep over the edge and you can still see the rusted metal ladder that descends into the depths but don't get too close.

As can be seen, the floor of the burn has been worked intensively. Open cast working on the east side of the burn operated from 1915 to 1925, extracting fluorspar which was then shipped via the Weardale Iron Company Railway. The water levels of the burn must have given some cause for concern during

28

The old shaft at Park Burn and, inset, the metal ladder going down into the depths.

The working on the lead vein.

the working, a short distance upstream a small dam has been constructed and the flow of water from it is directed by concrete channels and metal pipes down past the working site. Presumably this was to stop flooding of both the shaft and opencast workings when water levels were high.

3. From the side of the burn bear right to follow the path through the trees and up the side of the embankment to re-join the track bed and continue along the line. The workings of the Heights Quarry are now on the left of the track and after a little distance you'll pass a sign, laid on the floor at the time of test walking, warning of the dangers of the quarry. Follow the track bed as it heads towards a building, the reception and office buildings of the quarry, and here follow the fenced path past them. A few metres after the buildings the path comes to the side of the quarry's access road, next to the large safety sign, and here cross the road to a waymarked gate on the other side where the track continues. The old track bed is still very distinctive so follow this to a very wonky stile over a fence and then over the broken fence in front and along the track bed which is now fenced on both sides. **GR 930 390.**

Heights Quarry.

4. Continue to follow the old track bed, at times it goes through cuttings where, in order to keep your feet dry, you may have to go up the side of the bank. There are a couple of fences to cross, some with stiles, some without. The track bed is actually going round the side of the Heights Quarry and at times breaks in the left hand wall give you the opportunity to see the inside of it. After a while you'll go over a new stile to cross over a vehicle track before commencing on the track bed again. At this point if you look over to the right, to the skyline on the opposite side of the valley, you'll see the Elephant Trees walking proudly across the horizon. Shortly after this the rail line reaches the open moor where it runs along the side of the hill and you get your first glimpses of the Rookhope valley. The line crosses a large embankment over Sunderland Cleugh before curving round to the right to go round the side of the fell.

As the track passes the derelict farmhouse of High Bishopseat, look to the

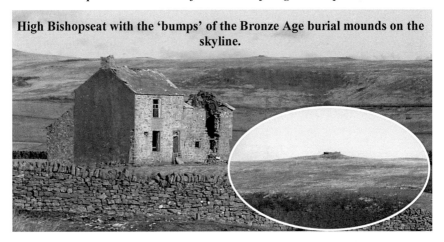

High Bishopseat with the 'bumps' of the Bronze Age burial mounds on the skyline.

skyline on the opposite side of the Rookhope valley to see three cairns, the middle one being the larger. These are burial cairns dating back to the Bronze Age over four thousand years ago. The fact that they are still quite visible after all these years of erosion proves that they were very effective at one of their functions, marking out the boundaries of the tribes people who built them.

The track bed now starts to slowly descend through farmland passing through gates and running down the side of a plantation as it heads towards Smailsburn Farm. As you can tell, the bed of the old rail line is now used as a track by the farmer and just before reaching the farm is joined by another track coming in from the right. Continue straight ahead passing through the farm and continuing to descend. As you approach Rookhope the land on either side of the track bed becomes more scarred from it's industrial use in the past and as you arrive opposite the village you'll pass a number of industrial buildings, which mark the site of the old Boltsburn Mine, before you arrive at a track junction with a bridge over the Rookhope Burn on the right. **GR 937 428.**

5. Don't cross the bridge and also ignore the track going straight ahead, instead turn left up the side of the wooden building and head for the visible marker post. Once there, ignore the marker pointing to the right and go straight ahead up the steps and follow the obvious path as it bears slightly to the right and heads up-hill making for the building in front. At the building turn left to go past it and follow the wall and, ignoring the stile and the marker post, keep the wall on your right as you start the steady climb up the hill. After a while you'll come to a wall corner. **GR 935 424.**

The small reservoir on the side of the hill.

6. Continue following the wall as it bends to come to the embanked sides of a small reservoir built to provide a source of water for the lead industry in the valley below. On the left side of the reservoir a stiles takes you over the fence in front and from here recommence following the wall on the right. As you climb up the hill it's worth stopping for the odd glance at the views behind. Over to the north the remains of the long flue from Rookhope Smelt Mill can be seen snaking their way up the side of the hill. Now it's just a case of following the wall on the right up the side of the hill, along the way you'll have to cross several fences, some have stiles, some don't and on these you'll have to cross the wooden fencing at the wall corner. Along the way a strange shape will appear over on the right, close to the summit of the hill. All will be revealed when you finally get to the top. Eventually you'll come to the last fence and here cross and as the wall you've followed now turns to the right, turn to follow it the few hundred metres up to the wall corner that is the top of the hill. The trig point that marks the summit is on the other side of the wall, it's top can be just seen above the stones. The mysterious shape is also now revealed as an observation hut built on stilt legs. **GR 917 413.**

The trig point on Windy Hill.

7. From the trig point continue following the wall on the right, which changes to a fence, across the summit plateau. This is quite boggy and water logged so you may have to jump around a bit to find the dry spots. When you get to the cross wall in front turn left to follow it back down the hill. The skeleton of an railway wagon appears over to the left and you'll then come to a wall corner and below it a track. Turn right to follow the track along what was once a walled lane, the lane is shown on the OS map as the Red Road and passes above the disused Marden Quarry. After passing through a gate the lane arrives at the roadside. **GR 912 405.**

8. Turn left onto the road and follow it back down the side of the valley, back to Westgate. The walk down the road is a pretty lengthy one but the road is quiet with not many vehicles to trouble you and the views over the valley take some beating. In particular take a look over to the right where the valley of the Middlehope Burn runs, this was one of the most important lead mining sites in Weardale and the shape of the landscape shows it. But that is a walk for another day.

Part-way down the road you'll come across an information board placed on the left hand side by the county council. This spot overlooks West Rigg Open Cut and the board explains a few details and identifies what can be seen.

West Rigg Open Cut.

West Rigg Open Cut is possibly the most impressive working in Weardale and is a site of special scientific interest. The site was originally worked by the Weardale Iron Company in the 1880's extracting the flat ironstone deposits. This left the large vein standing exposed in the middle of the open cut from which the lead ore was taken leaving the large slit down the face of the vein. Although the open cut is on the left side of the road, the vein itself did not stop here and continued over on the other side of the road. It's worth a look over the right side to see the workings there.

THE WEARDALE IRON COMPANY RAILWAY

The need for a modern transport system to move the mineral wealth of Weardale to market was recognised in the early 1800's and in 1834 the railways first reached the dale with the completion of the Stanhope and Tyne Railway which linked Stanhope with South Shields on the River Tyne. This line eventually becoming part of the Stockton and Darlington Railway in 1845.

Seeing the potential of the railway to move the vast iron ore deposits of the Rookhope and Middlehope valleys, the Weardale Iron Company approached the S&DR to build an extension of their line over to Rookhope. This request was refused leaving the iron company to build it's own line from a junction with the S&DR line at Parkhead, over the open moor near the summit of Bolts Law and down into Rookhope. This was completed by 1847.

The extension to this line over to the Middlehope valley above Westgate was started not long after. From Rookhope this extension turned south to Smailsburn after which the long climb up the side of the fell required the use of an incline worked by counterbalance, the weight of something heavy coming down the incline helping to pull the wagons up the slope. The weight used for the counterbalance was an old engine tender, the volume of water within the tender being changed to adjust it's weight, heavier to pull wagons up the incline and lighter

Looking down from the top of the Incline near High Bishopseat.

35

to let them back down again. From the top of the incline near High Bishopseat, the line ran almost level round the side of the fell to Scutter Hill above Westgate. Here it crossed the road and entered the Slitt Pasture ironstone mine. The track bed for this extension was completed by 1855.

The extension proved to be such a success that by the late 1850's, not only was it handling the output of the Middlehope mines but there was a continuous line of carts carrying iron and lead ore from the mines higher up the dale, up the 1 in 5 gradient of Scutter Hill to the loading point of the railway. The route that the carts climbed is along the road on which you came out of Westgate, at the start of the walk. It was tough enough walking up the steep gradient of the road, imagine horses pulling full loads of iron and lead ore up there when the road was still only a rough track.

The gradient of this hill presented a serious problem to the movement of the ore and to overcome this a spur line was built from the main line down to Westgate about 1860. A stationary steam engine hauled wagons of ore up the incline for onward shipment to Rookhope and beyond thus removing the need for horse drawn transport. Eventually in 1895 a new railway was built along the valley floor by the North Eastern Railway and this meant the end of the incline as there was no longer a need to take the ore up Scutter Hill.

By the 1870's the mines of the Rookhope and Middlehope valleys were transporting 30,000 tons of ore per year out of Rookhope and over the moors. However, not long after this the lead market collapsed and the industry went into terminal decline. While other parts of the line within the upper part of the Rookhope valley were no longer needed, the Heights Limestone Quarry, which was owned by the Weardale Iron Company, ensured that the Middlehope extension was still in full use.

During the First World War, the increased demand for iron and steel ensured a high demand for limestone which was used in it's manufacture. Production at Heights Quarry was high but the volume that could be transported out was limited due to the steep climb of the Bolt's Law Incline on the exit from Rookhope. To overcome this bottleneck, an incline was constructed from the quarry down to the NER line that ran along the valley floor. In a stroke the need to run the rail line over the moors was removed and it was only a question of time before the use of the extension was ended.

Small, diminishing quantities were still transported over to Rookhope but by the early 1920's the line was idle. It was officially closed in 1923 with the metal tracks being lifted for scrap in 1943. Now the track bed provides a very pleasant green track, albeit slightly boggy in places, along which to walk along the side of the dale.

Heading up to the Lang Man O'Bollihope.
Walk 3. The Bollihope Watershed.

WALK 3: THE BOLLIHOPE WATERSHED

A walk high along the watershed of the Bollihope valley, among the peat hags and streamlets that feed down into the burn and, ultimately, the River Wear itself. Don't be fooled by the distance and height gained on this walk, it is more tiring than they would suggest due to the ups and downs of the peat hags and the extra distance put in walking round the worst of the boggy ground. However that said, this is a walk that you could get a lot of satisfaction out of completing, especially, if you take a break at the trig point on Harnisha Hill. From this vantage point you can look out and trace almost the full route of the walk across the skyline as it circles round above the valley.

This walk also gives you the extra of a visit to see the cairn of the Lang Man O'Bollihope, reputably the grave of a giant warrior.

DISTANCE: 9.4 miles / 15 km.
ASCENT: 1,220 feet / 372 metres.
TERRAIN: Mainly pathless high-level moor complete with it's share of peat bogs. The final stretch is a 3 km road walk down the B6278 back to the car.
TIME: 4 to 5 hours.
START: Parking space alongside the B6278 road on the north side of the Bollihope Burn. GR NY 985 352.
MAP: Explorer OL31 North Pennines.
DOGS: Not permitted on the open access land.
ACCESS: The route is entirely over open access land.

GRID REFERENCES:

Parking space	985 352
Bollihope Cairn	964 356
Fence	945 347
Fence corner	941 332
Road	992 319
Lang Man O'Bollihope	996 318
Parking space	985 352

FGS GRADING:
Grading is F11 [D1, N2, T3, R3,H2]

Distance	1	6 – 12 miles
Navigation	2	Competent navigation skills needed
Terrain	3	Under 25% on graded track or path Over 75% off track
Remoteness	3	Remote, isolated location
Height	2	Over 125 ft per mile

Catterick and the Bollihope Valley from Bollihope Carrs.

39

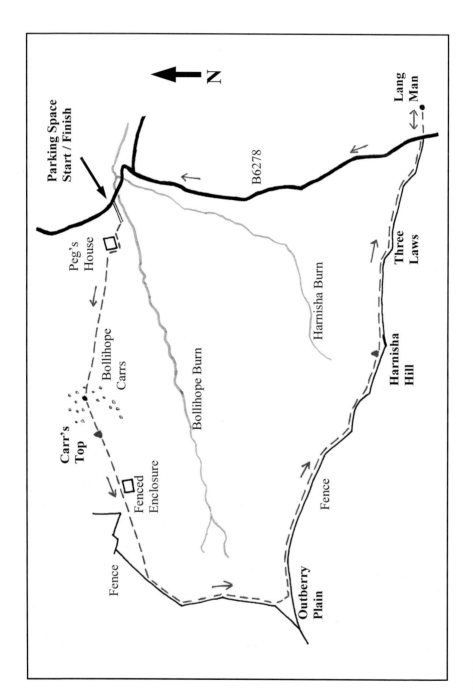

THE WALK

1. From the start at the side of the road there are three vehicle tracks heading away from the parking area. Take the middle track as it curves it's way uphill.

The three tracks at the start of the walk.

After a short distance a walled compound comes into view. Follow the track as it heads towards it and make your way round the left side of the walls to come to the top left hand corner of the enclosure.

The walled enclosure is known as Peg's House and beneath it's turf are the remains of a Romano-British farmstead dating back to the first century.

From the corner of the walled compound as you look towards the north west, a stone cairn can be seen on the skyline. Head straight uphill across the open moor towards it, crossing two streams as you go. The cairn is just over 1.5 km away and is steady climbing all the way. Just before the cairn you cross a farmer's quad bike track and then enter the boulder field of Bollihope Carrs. Cross the boulder field to come to the cairn. **GR 964 356.**

2. From the cairn bear south west following the crest of the ridge and after a short distance come to the trig point on Carrs Top.

Standing at only 540 metres, Carrs Top is not particularly high but it is one of my favourite viewpoints in the whole of the Durham Dales. It's positioning between the Bollihope Burn and Weardale plus the way that the land is shaped and falls away to the east just gives me a buzz every time that I come up here.

Heading up the slopes towards Bollihope Carrs.

Continue following the crest of the ridge as it climbs in a rough south westerly direction. After approximately 800 metres, you'll pass a small fenced enclosure on the left and shortly afterwards an old railway wagon. About this time, a stone wall starts to become visible on the right and begins to run parallel with you. As you climb higher, the route starts to traverse a number of peat hags and then you'll arrive at a fence line. Because of the need to negotiate the peat hags, it is unlikely that you will meet the fence at exactly this grid reference but you shouldn't be too far out. **GR 945 347.**

3. Turn left to follow the fence and you now keep it on your right as it slowly climbs over Snowhope Hill on it's way to Outberry Plain. This stretch of the walk traverses the head of the valley, above the multitude of small water courses that drain from these peat bogs and flow down to create the Bollihope Burn. After 1.5 km of bog hopping, the fence reaches it's high spot just below the summit of Outberry Plain and here it comes to a very sharply angled fence corner before coming back out on itself again. At this point it is possible to cut the corner by heading across the peat rather than going all the way into the corner and then coming back out again. **Fence corner GR 941 332.**

4. Continue following the fence line as it now starts to slowly descend from Outberry Plain. This is a bit of a long slog but the trig point on Harnisha Hill eventually comes into view. Unfortunately just before reaching it, the route descends into a shallow col which gives you a slight climb up to the concrete pillar. It's worth spending some time at the trig point, maybe have a cup of tea and

Bog-hopping along the watershed.

a sandwich. Here you are almost exactly opposite the trig point on Carrs Top with the whole of the valley laid out between you. From the trig point continue following the fence line down over Three Laws to come to the roadside of the B6278. **GR 992 319.**

5. Cross the road and follow the path that runs next to the line of old fence posts and up the short climb to the stone cairn of the Lang Man O' Bollihope. **GR 996 318.** Return back to the road the same way.

6. At the road turn right, to follow the B6278 back down into the Bollihope valley. There is now just over 3 km of road walking to get back to the car but the good news is, it is downhill all the way.

THE LANG MAN O'BOLLIHOPE

One clear summer's evening, many, many years ago, two tall figures were seen to meet on the black ridge of Bollihope and immediately began a mortal battle. The clash of their weapons was heard far off in the valley and to the onlookers far below the two warring figures that were set against the night sky reminded them of the giants from the days of old.

For hours the two figures fought, backwards and forwards along the ridge until at last one of them was seen to fall. The triumphant victor proclaimed his success and then after a short space of time, vanished as mysteriously as the two figures had appeared.

The next morning, the local inhabitants plucked up their courage and braved the site. There was no trace of the victor of the momentous struggle but on top of the ridge lay the remains of the vanquished, the mangled corpse of a very tall man.

No-one knew the name of the mysterious warrior who lay dead at their feet and no-one came forward to claim his earthly remains. These were laid to rest where he fell and a pile of stones were raised over the grave to mark the spot. The stones now mark the resting place of the Lang Man O' Bollihope.

Weardale Folklore.

The cairn and boundary stone of the Lang Man O'Bollihope.

Sometimes a monument can be in place for so long that it becomes part of folklore and tradition. The stone cairn on the ridge above Bollihope is one of these. No-one knows when or why the cairn was first raised, as the saying goes that 'is lost in the mists of antiquity' but the stones are of a considerable age and the spot itself has become named after the cairn and this has been transferred across to the modern Ordnance Survey map although they have used the correct English rather than the local pronunciation.

The prominent location of the site along the Teesdale/Weardale watershed has also meant that it has served a later pur-pose of acting as a boundary and a carved boundary stone from the 17/18th century stands alongside the stone mound. Some more modern curricks have been built a short distance from the Lang Man cairn. These make for an interesting little diversion as they give some outstanding views out over Teesdale.

The age of the Lang Man cairn is not known and there is no documentation of any excavation of the site. There is the possibility that it may be the remains of a Bronze Age burial mound, artefacts from this period have been found in the Bollihope valley below, but this is unlikely. The stronger possibility is that it is much more modern and was originally intended as a marker cairn to indicate the route of the road that lies below it.

Although covered in tarmac now, this road has existed as a transport corridor probably since pre-Roman days. Large sections of the modern road are laid on top of a Roman road linking Teesdale and Weardale. The Roman road itself may have possibly made use of an even earlier passageway, surprisingly the Teesdale end arrives relatively close to the site of the Eggleston Neolithic stone circle, which sadly no longer remains. However, there is no evidence of a link between the two and any connection may be just purely circumstantial.

**Looking back down the track to the
North Grains Beck.**

WALK 4: BACK O' FIVE PIKES

This is a walk that traverses the western slopes of Five Pikes and the expansive open moorland of Pikestone Fell. Being not very high, these hills can be quite deceptive as they offer far-sweeping views to distant horizons. Throughout the walk this route utilises the well-laid out system of shooter's tracks established over this moor by the Bollihope Estate.

DISTANCE: 10.6 miles / 17 km
ASCENT: 919 feet / 280 metres
TERRAIN: The majority of the route is on well-surfaced moorland track. There is one stretch along a well-walked moorland path and the final stretch from Blackburn Lodge follows a quiet tarmac lane.
TIME: 4 to 5 hours.
START: Parking space at the top of West Bank above Wolsingham, at the start of the minor road leading to Blackburn Lodge and Doctor's Gate. GR NZ 073 357.
MAP: Explorer OL31 North Pennines.
DOGS: Not permitted on the open access land.
ACCESS: Most of this route follows shooter's tracks over open access land.

GRID REFERENCES:

Parking space	073 357
Path/track junction	063 349
Track junction	025 356
Path/track junction	011 327
Track crossroads	026 328
Track junction	031 327
Track junction	045 335
Doctor's Gate	071 329
Parking space	073 357

FGS GRADING:
Grading is F4 [D1, N1, T0, R2,H0]

Distance	1	6 – 12 miles
Navigation	1	Basic navigation skills needed
Terrain	0	75% + on graded track or path
Remoteness	2	Countryside not in close proximity to habitation – less than 20% of the route within 2 miles
Height	0	Less than 100 ft per mile

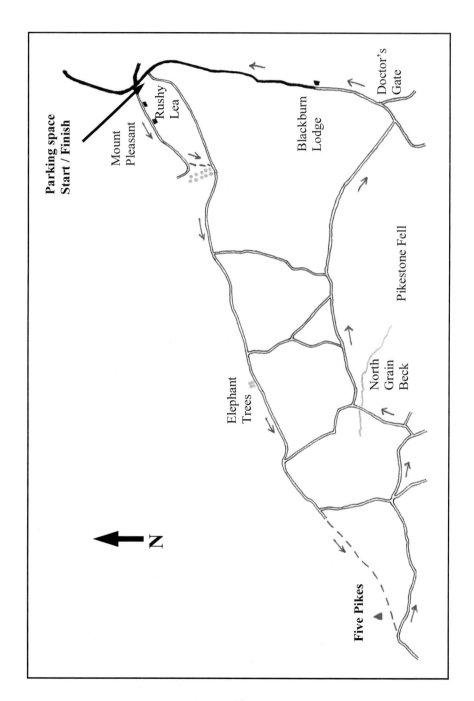

N

Parking space
Start / Finish

Mount
Pleasant

Rushy
Lea

Blackburn
Lodge

Doctor's
Gate

Pikestone Fell

Elephant
Trees

North
Grain
Beck

Five Pikes

THE WALK

1. From the car parking space, head back down the road towards Wolsingham and after a short distance turn left up the walled track leading to Carr's Farm as shown by the bridleway sign.

The start of the walk, heading down to the Wolsingham road and the track to Carr's Farm.

Follow the track past the cottages of Rushy Lea and Mount Pleasant. Shortly after the second cottage, the track goes through a gate into a field, the wall on the right disappears and the wall on the left turns away from the track. At this point leave the track and follow the wall on the left to a gate in the wall corner. Go through the gate and then head diagonally uphill across the field making for a gate in the wall next to the top end of the belt of trees that edge the field. Go through the gate onto a track. **GR 063 349.**

2. Once on the track, turn right and follow it through two gates to gain access to the open moor. Continue following the track as it runs on the left side of the wall for 2 km and past two junctions on the left. Approximately 400 metres after passing the second junction, come to a small clump of trees that stand on the right side of the wall.

These are the famous Elephant Trees that stand above Weardale and which are highly visible from many parts of the dale. They are named the Elephant Trees because, from a distance, they closely resemble a troop of elephants walking nose to tail across the skyline.

Following the track to the Elephant Trees and, inset, the Trees.

Continue following the track and
you'll soon come to a junction where a
Weardale Way marker post points
down a track that heads through a gate
in the right hand wall. Ignore this and continue on your original track as it
makes it's way along the outside of the wall. You'll soon come to yet another
junction, this time with a track on the left that heads off across the moor. Stay
following the wall until you come to a another junction. **GR 025 356.**

3. Continue following the track alongside the wall and it very quickly becomes a
moorland path and then leaves the wall to head towards two marker posts, the
further one being visible on the skyline. Follow this moorland path as it skirts
round the high ground of Five Pikes over on the right. The path is marked by
periodic marker posts and although thin, is fairly easy to follow. Once past Five
Pikes the path joins a well-constructed vehicle track. **GR 011 327.**

4. Turn left to follow the track as it heads over to the wide expanse of Pikestone
Fell. Along the way you'll pass one of the old railway carriages that lie dotted
across these moors. After just over 1 km you'll come to a crossroads of tracks.
GR 026 328. Continue straight ahead and after 800 metres you'll come to a
track junction. **GR 031 327.**

The moors up here on the Bollihope Estate are pretty well served by a network of tracks that give access for the grouse shooters. They used to be inaccessible but since the introduction of the CRoW Act, walkers can now quite happily use them. The walks over these tracks provide some great scenery with the wide, open areas of the moors flowing down to the trees of Hamsterley Forest.

5. Turn left at the junction and after a short distance go past another junction on the right. The track will now start heading down hill to cross the North Grains Beck but don't worry you won't get your feet wet. Just after the crossing, there is a track junction but here follow the main track as it bears round to the right and starts to climb up from the side of the beck. Continue following the track until you come to yet another junction. **GR 045 335.**

As you climb up away from the North Grains Beck think to look back. Sometimes the best views are behind you.

6. At the junction turn right onto another well-made track. As you progress you'll pass through an area of old workings and here you'll find yet another of the redundant railway wagons that seem to populate these moors. As you pass through the workings, you'll no-

Following the shooter's track across Pikestone Fell.

tice one or two tracks heading off to the side but it is easy to tell which is the main track, so just stay on it. Eventually the track comes to a wall corner and then starts to run along the outside of the wall for the next 1.25 km. At the end of the wall there is a minor track going off to the right but continue following the main track round to the left to come to a track junction in front of a gate. This is Doctor's Gate. **GR 071 329.**

7. Go through the gate and follow the partially surfaced track straight ahead. Shortly you'll go through another gate and here you'll pass Blackburn Lodge on the right. By now the track has become a tarmac road and this is now followed for the next 2 km to arrive back at the start point and the car.

**Looking downstream from West Blackdene bridge.
Walk 5. Wearhead and Sedling Rake.**

WALK 5: WEARHEAD AND SEDLING RAKE

A walk of two distinct halves. The first following the Weardale Way along the valley floor upstream from St John's Chapel to Wearhead, at times walking close to the riverbank while at other times a field or so away from the river. The second half of the walk from Wearhead back to St John's Chapel climbs up the side of the fell and follows an old packhorse track along the edge of the valley which, on a nice day, gives some superb views of the dale before it descends back down to the valley floor.

DISTANCE: 7.2 mile / 11.5 km
ASCENT: 1,004 feet / 306 metres
TERRAIN: A walk of two halves. The first half up to Wearhead utilises field and riverbank paths, most of which are quite well walked. From Wearhead the route climbs the side of the valley, some of which can be quite steep, to return to St Johns Chapel by moorland tracks and paths. Some of these moorland tracks and paths can be quite wet and muddy in places even during summer. A short stretch following a bridleway from Queensbury up to the Sedling Rake track is more of a faint path across open moor but while a bit rough underfoot, is fairly easy to negotiate as there is a wall nearby to guide you.
TIME: 4½ to 5 hours
START: The large car parking area on the east side of St Johns Chapel, just before you enter the village. GR NY 886 379
MAP: OL31 North Pennines
DOGS: As this route is all on public rights of way then dogs are allowed. However, keep them under close control and on a lead, especially when going through the areas of old mine workings as there are old shafts, levels and other holes in the ground. Livestock will be encountered throughout the route and there are a couple of farmyards that you pass through where other dogs will definitely be encountered.
ACCESS: This route is all on public rights of way.

GRID REFERENCES
Car Park	886 379
Path crossroads	885 383
Coronation Bridge	873 386
West Blackdene Bridge	867 391
Wearhead	858 395
Road	858 402

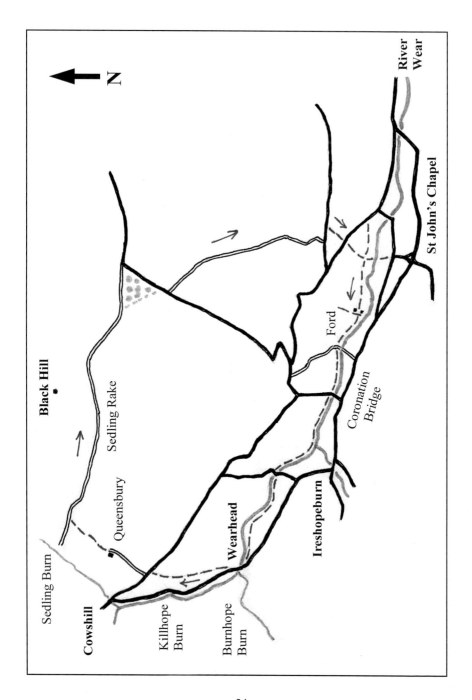

Path/track junction	862 410
Road corner	884 405
Road	887 387
Car park	886 379

FGS GRADING:
Grading is F5 [D1, N1, T0, R1,H2]

Distance	1	6 – 12 miles
Navigation	1	Basic navigation skills needed
Terrain	0	75% + on graded track or path
Remoteness	1	Countryside in fairly close proximity to habitation – at least 80% of the route within 2 miles
Height	2	Over 125 ft per mile

THE WALK

1. Leave the car parking space to go past the Golden Lion and into the village. After a few metres turn right down the side road, following the sign for St Johns Chapel Primary School, and pass the town hall on the left. At the bottom of the village, where the road bends right, turn left up the smaller minor road for a few

Head down the side-road passing the town hall on it's little patch of green.

metres to a footpath signpost. Here leave the road to turn right to a waymarked gate and enter a small field where the path goes ahead but bearing slightly to the left to come to the river and the Ponderlane footbridge. Cross the bridge and go straight ahead for about 100 metres to come to a ruined wall and a footpath signpost indicating a path crossroads. **GR 885 383.**

2. Here turn left to follow the right side of the ruined wall to a visible stile a short distance away. When you get to the stile you'll find that it has waymarkers for the Minerals Valley Walk which point to the right, ignore these and head straight across the narrow field to a stile opposite. This is the first in a sequence of narrow fields where you go through a combination of stiles and kissing gates which, as you cross, are always visible on the opposite side of the field. Although not really marked as such, at this point the path that you are following forms part of the Weardale Way, the route of this long distance path now being followed to Wearhead.

After a couple of fields, you'll approach a farm and here you'll find the stile next to the gate on the right of the house. Cross the stile and go straight ahead passing the right side of the house and going down a small, short lane that takes you behind the buildings to a small gate with a red disk on it. Go through into the field and follow the fence on the left. The field lies next to, but above the riverbank and after a short while you'll approach a footbridge going over the river. When you get to the bridge you'll find a stile on the left leading onto the bridge and a lane. Cross the stile but ignore the bridge and continue along the right side of the river, following the markers along the bank and passing the waterfall with the ford running along the top of it. Follow the well-trodden river-

The small waterfall and ford.

56

side path to eventually come to the Coronation Bridge where a stile at the side of it brings you out on the roadside. **GR 873 386.**

Cross the road and continue to follow the riverside path on the other side of the bridge.

As you walk along the path keep your eyes open for sharp movements in and around the water. This stretch is a favourite for Dippers and this little black and white bird can be fascinating to watch as it bobs in and out of the water.

It's not long before the path passes beneath a concrete bridge where, on the other side of the river, the Ireshope Burn joins the main stream. You only go a little way past the bridge before the path joins a track which runs along the side of the river. At this point the river bed has been worn down to the bedrock and the river rushes down in a series of small waterfalls and cataracts. The track now approaches the small hamlet of West Blackdene where, once again, you come to a road next to a bridge. **GR 867 391.**

As you approach West Blackdene you'll be able to see the distinctive shape of a railway bridge on the other side of the river. This may seem an odd place to see a railway bridge but it formed part of the Weardale Line operated by the London and North Eastern Railway and which ran up to Wearhead. The flat level ground of the old track bed can be easily seen on the other bank of the river as it males it's way up to the bridge.

Approaching West Blackdene. Inset, the old railway bridge.

3. At the roadside turn left to cross the bridge over the river and once across immediately turn right to leave the road and go down the track indicated by the marker post passing through the gate for Waterside Farm. Follow the track to the farm and go through the two small gates on the right side of it to emerge behind the buildings. A sequence of marker posts now guide you through the riverside fields. At one point you cross a small lane, ignoring the bridge across the river on your right. After a short while the path will approach some houses where it exits onto the roadside. Turn right to cross the road bridge over the river and enter Wearhead. **GR 858 395.**

The River Wear is unusual among northern rivers in that it doesn't have a single source gushing from some lonely spring high on the hillside. Instead it is born of a confluence of a number of streams here at Wearhead. Look from the upstream side of the bridge and you'll see the waters of the Burnhope Burn and the Killhope Burn mingling together.

4. Follow the road through the hamlet and approximately 100 metres after leaving the bridge you'll come to a faded bridleway sign, partially hidden by a lamppost, on the left side of the road pointing up a lane on the right side. Turn right up the lane and after a few metres this opens out onto a wide space and here turn left to follow a track uphill past the houses. There are no markers here to indicate that this is a bridleway even though it has all the appearances of an old walled lane. At the last house the gravel track ends but continue straight ahead

As you walk up the track you are presented with some great views up to the high fells of the dale.

on what is now a green lane. The track continues climbing up above the valley of the Killhope Burn at the same time giving some good views of the high fells of the upper dale. After a short while you'll come to a gate, go through and continue straight ahead to come to a second gate. Once through this gate, bear right to follow a path that goes steeply up the bank on that side to come to a small red gate in the wall above. When you are through the gate, follow the faint but distinctive path that goes ahead but bearing slightly to the left. Once over the rise make for the marker post next to the gate to exit out onto the roadside. **GR 858 402.**

5. Turn left to follow the road for a 100 metres or so to come to a lane on the right side with a bridleway sign pointing up it and a post box for Queensbury at it's entrance. Head up the lane, passing through a gate just before you get to the farm. When you get to the building, go through two small gates to the right of the house and once past, make for the gate in front that leads onto the open moor. Go through the gate and follow a narrow path that goes straight ahead following the wall on the right. After a short distance the path moves slightly away from the wall and soon comes to the side of a small gully where it has to descend to cross the stream at the bottom before climbing up the other side again. A trackway now becomes visible a short distance away in front and the path is heading towards it. However, before it gets there it comes to a wide,

The heavily scarred side of the Sedling Burn valley.

deep gully which in reality is an old hush and the location of the High Sedling Mine Level. Descend to the bottom of the hush and turn right to follow it uphill to arrive at the entrance to the level. **GR 862 410.**

Looking down and along the hush and, inset, the level entrance.

From the level there is an obvious track that leads round the front of the hill and within a few metres meets the well-constructed track that you have seen for the last few minutes. **GR 862 410.**

6. Turn right to follow the track as it makes it's way uphill. Within metres the track bends to the left and here crosses a leat, a man-made water channel that flows beneath the track. The stonework can still be seen supporting the track. As you climb ignore the lesser track that turns off left and stay with the main track that bears right to come to a gate complete with waymarker. As you have climbed the track has kept close company with the Sedling Vein.

The path of this ore vein is marked by the deep gash in the ground where the ore was extracted by hushing and open cast workings. As you walk alongside it, picture it as it was then full of noise and dirt with men using hammer, pick and shovel to separate the ore from the rock. The vein is worked all the way up to the top of the fell, As you get higher the open cast workings are replaced by deep shafts as the vein loses touch with the surface and continues underneath the hill.

The deep workings at the side of the track and, inset, the metal rail embedded in the ground.

Go through the gate and continue on the track as it climbs with the old workings over on the left. After a short while, a gate is passed through and here lies another reminder of the old lead days, a short section of metal rail upon which the tubs of ore were pushed is left embedded in the ground. The track is now accompanied by a line of old shafts on the left. Stay with the track as it continues to climb, albeit not so steeply now, and runs along the side of the hill giving superb views of the valley and the hills on it's southern side.

The track that you are following is the old packhorse route from the mines at the head of the valley, over and across the moors to the ore smelters at Rookhope. Weardale was the last place in northern England to still use packhorses for the lead trade even long after the railway came to the valley. The mines at the top end of the dale were so remote that the continued use of the pony was essential. Packhorse trains of twenty five Galloway ponies, each animal carrying two pokes of ore, about 224 lbs. or 102 kg, moved constantly back and forwards across these hills.

The track heading down past the wood to the road and, inset, fluorspar from the track.

The OS map shows this track running along the edge of Sedling Rake. The word 'Rake' is the old miner's term for vein, meaning that this is the course of the Sedling Lead Vein.

As the gradient of the track levels out you may notice a purple tinge to the surface of the track. Purple fluorspar quartz lies scattered along it, dropped from the panniers of the packhorses. It's not long before the summit of Black Hill can be seen over on the left and shortly after this, a wall comes in on the left and you arrive at a double gate next to some sheep pens. Go through the gates and here the track becomes enclosed. Continue down past a small wood, and here, once again, the purple sheen of the fluorspar becomes prominent again, to come to a road corner. **GR 884 405.**

7. The old packhorse trail continues straight on towards Rookhope, the route now being the tarmac road but here is where you leave it to turn right and follow the other branch of the road downhill for a couple of hundred metres, passing the end of the wood on the way, to come to a walled lane on the left side of the road with a bridleway sign pointing along it. Leave the road to go down the lane and when you get to the bottom, go through the gate and follow the left hand wall, passing some old shafts on the way, to come to another gate. Go through to enter another walled lane and follow this down to come to a roadside. **GR 887 387.**

8. From the roadside both St Johns Chapel and the route down through the fields can be clearly seen. However, if you look in the fields directly below you, the shape of a prehistoric stone circle can be seen, it's vertical stones standing proudly in the middle of the field. Don't be fooled, this is actually a modern reconstruction made from old stone gateposts but it does look the business. You do end up on the track in the field next to the circle so there is the opportunity for a closer look.

Turn left for a short distance to the footpath sign on the right side of the road and here cross the stile into the field and follow the direction of the sign to cross diagonally down the field to a gap in the wall on the right. Cross and, again, go diagonally down the field to a stile next to a gateway which, in turn, leads onto a track. Turn right to follow the track the short distance down onto the road.

If you fancied a look, the stone circle lies in the field on the right and can easily be seen over the wall.

Cross the road to follow the footpath on the other side, down over the field making for the end of the fence and the handrail that can be seen amongst the trees. Follow the steps down and then go straight ahead to Ponderlane bridge. Cross, go over the field to the road, turn left to the junction and then turn right to go back up to the main road where you turn left back to the parking space..

THE SEDLING BURN VALLEY

Within the valley of the Sedling Burn, four major lead veins converge along with a number of smaller veins and a sizeable deposit of ironstone and where all of these meet, the surface of the valley has been plundered by mining activity to the point where there is very little of the original land surface untouched. As you can see from the side of the valley, the whole area is scarred by numerous small hushes and the workings from the shafts used to reach the iron and lead.

Three of the lead veins, Breckonsike, Burtree Pasture and Coptcleugh were worked from the Burtree Pasture Mine using shafts and four levels. The fourth vein, Sedling, the line of which is followed on this walk, was worked by the Sedling Mine using all three methods of extraction, levels, shafts and opencut. On the valley floor, down below the buildings of Queensbury, the ironstone was extracted from the west side of the burn via the Queensbury Ironstone Workings.

The earliest record of mining in the valley comes from 1425 when workings on the Burtree Pasture Vein were recorded although some form of mining was going on long before this. By the 1860/70's over 200 men were being employed by the Burtree Pasture Mine and from 1818 to 1876, the mine produced over a third of the ore taken from Weardale.

As with many other mines in the dale, Burtree Pasture became idle with the collapse of the lead industry in the late 1800's. However, the mine was reopened in the 1970's to extract fluorspar but was closed again by 1981.

The Sedling Vein runs from the east side of the burn and was worked very intensively. A large opencut follows the line of the vein up the side of the hill, this being created by hushing very early in the working of the vein. Along the top of the hill a line of old shafts follow the vein as excavations were made to access the deeper deposits, these linking to levels driven into the side of the valley.

The workings were in existence in 1720 with around 70 men being employed. This had risen to 139 men by 1788 but by the early 1800's had fallen to about 50.

High Sedling Mine Level was a later attempt at accessing the ore, being driven in 1926 by a Sheffield based company, Messrs Hinchcliffe. During the short life of this level, nearly 5,000 tons of ore were produced from the mine.

Following the road down from Allotment House.

WALK 6: PAWLAW PIKE

On the southern side of the Bollihope valley the slopes gently rise to a vast expanse of low-lying moorland. A small crest-line is formed by the hills of Long Man, Pawlaw Pike and Five Pikes, after which the heather moor continues to stretch away south to break upon the timber borders of Hamsterley Forest several miles distant. This is the land of the red grouse reared, as in many other parts of the Durham uplands, to face the gun during the shooting season.

In recent times the whole nature of these uplands has changed with the demands of the shooting estates. What was once open moor now contains long, sweeping vehicle tracks which provide access for shooters and gamekeepers. And then there is the moor itself, now a patchwork mosaic of heather beds where the new growth is stimulated by the controlled burning of the older plants. Whereas we think of these moorlands as being beautiful wild places, in fact they have been shaped by the hand of man just as much as any urban parkland.

DISTANCE: 7.5 miles / 12 km
ASCENT: 938 feet / 286 metres
TERRAIN: Initially well-surfaced vehicle track giving way to moorland path as you pass the hill of Five Pikes. The route does cross a short stretch of open moorland between the Fine Burn and Pye Close where there is very little in the way of paths.
TIME: 4 to 5 hours.
START: Car parking area next to the Bollihope Burn. GR NZ 006 349.
MAP: OL31 North Pennines.
DOGS: Not permitted on the open access land.
ACCESS: The initial part of the route uses public access land and then from Five Pikes onwards utilises public rights of way.

GRID REFERENCES:

Parking area	006 349
Track junction	003 331
Track/path junction	010 326
Five Pikes	013 329
Path/track junction	022 334
Track junction	036 341
Gate	029 048
Fine Burn	025 344
Pye Close	019 352
Parking area	006 349

FGS GRADING:
Grading is F6 [D1, N1, T1, R1,H2]

Distance	1	6 – 12 miles
Navigation	1	Basic navigation skills needed
Terrain	1	50 – 75% on graded track or path 25 – 50% off track
Remoteness	1	Countryside in fairly close proximity to habitation – at least 80% of the route within 2 miles
Height	2	Over 125 ft per mile

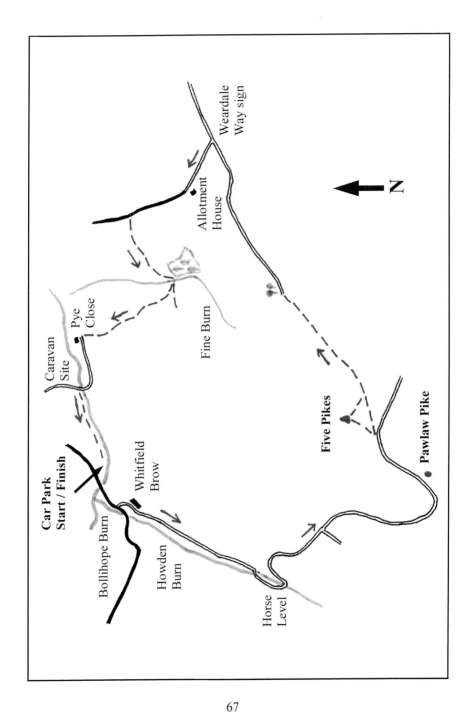

N

Car Park
Start / Finish

Bollihope Burn

Whitfield
Brow

Howden
Burn

Caravan
Site

Pye
Close

Fine Burn

Horse
Level

Five Pikes

Pawlaw Pike

Allotment
House

Weardale
Way sign

THE WALK

1. From the car parking area turn left onto the road and follow it as it crosses over the Bollihope Burn. After a couple of hundred metres turn left onto the tarmac track leading up to the houses on Whitfield Brow. Stay on the main track as it changes to an unmetaled surface and passes the houses, then go round a gate to continue on the track as it slowly climbs above the Howden Burn. Ignore the side track that you pass on the left and keep heading up the valley. Eventually the track crosses the burn and enters into an area of old mine workings before doing a sharp left to re-cross the burn and climb steeply up the side of the hill.

Approaching the old mine workings.

The workings on either side of the track were part of a complex of levels and shafts that worked the Cornish Hush Vein, which here crossed the Howden Burn. It is not known when the mines were started but they were in existence in 1791 when the lease was purchased by the Beaumont Company. Nor is the origin of the name known although Cornish tin miners did migrate north to work in the lead fields and the two may be connected. On the corner of the track was the entrance to Cornish Hush Horse Level, a horse level being the

entrance by which the ponies that worked the mines entered. Most mines had separate levels for the ponies that worked underground and these tended to be the better entrances. Although slightly larger than the normal levels, they were, more importantly, drier. Most levels also doubled as drainage for the mines and as a result usually had a constant stream of water flowing out of them, making them quite unpleasant to go in and out of.

The top of the level entrance buried by the spoil heap.

The top of the characteristic arch marking the entrance to the level can still be seen poking out of a bank of waste. In 1971 the level was re-opened for a short period to explore for fluorspar but this was unsuccessful. The whole area of the mine has been 're-landscaped' during these workings of the 1970's and it looks as if the burial of the level was part of this.

As the track levels out after the climb it passes a collection of sheep pens standing on the left and then comes to a junction. **GR 003 331.**

2. Follow the track straight ahead as it slowly climbs Pawlaw Pike. Just before it gets to the summit the track does a sharp left hand turn. Follow the track round and just off the track and to the right is the top of Pawlaw Pike, visible as the high ground. It's worth the short diversion over the heather for the views down to Hamsterley Forest before returning back to the track. Continue on the track until you come to the next bend where there is a small cairn and here a narrow path leaves the track. **GR 010 326.**

3. Leave the track but don't follow the path, instead head across the heather to the visible trig point on the top of Five Pikes just 300 metres straight ahead. **GR 013 329.**

The top of Five Pikes is a fairly wide area, a couple of hundred metres across. As well as the trig point there is also a stone cairn to the north west of the trig and another one to the south east. Both of them lie on the edge of the summit area and make good viewpoints over the surrounding moors.

4. After visiting the trig point head to the south eastern cairn and from there head due south to come to the narrow path that left the track and which has skirted round and below the summit of Five Pikes.

Heading away from the trig point towards the south eastern cairn.

Turn left onto the path and follow it as it heads away over the moor. The path is fairly distinctive and easy to follow and route finding is aided by the occasional marker post. If in any difficulty head towards the trees that can be seen in the distance behind a wall line. After 1.5 km the path joins the start of a track next to the trees and wall. **GR 022 334.**

5. Join onto the track and start following it as it makes it's way running along the outside of the wall. There are a couple of tracks on the right that head off over the moors but ignore these. Instead continue following the wall for 2 km until you come to the first gate set into the wall on the left. Here you will find a Weardale Way signpost indicating the way to White Kirkley. **GR 036 341.**

Joining the Weardale Way down to Allotment House.

6. Turn left to go through the gate and follow the direction of the signpost down the track to Allotment House which can be seen as the large building just below. At the house the track becomes a tarmac road, continue following this road as it descends and becomes enclosed by walls on either side. The road passes a couple of belts of trees before you come to the point where the wall on the left moves away from the road to create an open space and here a gate crosses the road in front. **GR 029 048.**

7. Go through the gate and immediately turn left to follow the right side of the wall through the trees. This is actually a bridleway but there is no signpost at the side of the road to indicate it. Follow the side of the wall and at the end of the trees come to a cross wall and gate. Go through the gate and head straight across the next field to come to a second gate on the opposite side. Pass through and then follow the rough track as it heads steeply downhill, curving to the left to come to a narrow gate leading down to a crossing of the Fine Burn. **GR 025 344.**

8. The side of the Fine Burn makes a good place to stop for a cup of tea with the tinkling of the water being quite hypnotic. The crossing of the stream is not that difficult, it is fairly shallow and there are plenty of stones to stand on. Once across, follow the track up the slope on the other side and at the top leave the track to follow a faint path on the right. This faint path makes it's way across the heather but it is very easily lost. Head round the shoulder of the hill and when it becomes visible, make for the white painted house of Pye Close. **GR 019 352.**

Heading round the side of the hill towards Pye Close.

9. In front of the house bear left along the track as indicated by the bridleway sign. The track soon goes through a gate and descends to the Bollihope Burn which it follows for a short distance to come to a ford that crosses the burn.

As you follow the track by the side of the burn, you'll pass the remains of an old lime kiln. Built during the 1700's this kiln is now a listed building. Under-rated by many, these lime kilns have had a significant impact on the land-scape of the dale, possibly as much as the impact of mining and quarrying but in a much more subtle way. On your walks have you ever wondered how a field can be full of grass suitable for grazing livestock and then right next to it, is open peat moorland. The answer is lime kilns, for centuries lime was produced from these kilns and then used as a top-dressing to 'sweeten' the grass of the fields. At one point virtually every farm in the dale had it's own kiln with an associated small quarry close by. Here limestone would be dug from the earth and then burnt in the kiln to produce quicklime which, mixed with water, was used as a fertiliser. This enrichment of the soil enabled many parts of the dale to be cultivated, without it many of the green fields that you see would have just been bleak moorland. The practice of lime burning has long been superseded by an alternative chemical process and these kilns, which were so formative of the landscape that we know today, just lie forgotten and ignored.

The now derelict lime kilns.

Here you have a route choice. The first option is to cross the ford in front of the caravan site and then bear left to follow the track upstream along the right bank back to the car park. Alternatively you can stay on the left bank of the burn and head upstream, making your way through the spoil heaps back to the road and here you use the road bridge to cross the burn back to the car park.

The track descending through the trees towards Fawnlees.

WALK 7: NEWLANDS AND FAWNLEES

A shorter distance walk that visits a part of the dale that is not so often frequented by walkers. A surprisingly pleasant walk that presents a range of environments for the walker.

DISTANCE: 4.75 miles / 7.5 km
ASCENT: 830 feet / 253 metres

TERRAIN: The route is almost entirely on field paths and tracks with a short stretch through woodland. There are no significant climbs on this route although there is one short, steep one.
TIME: 3 to 3½ hours.
START: Lay-by on the south side of the A689 road running from Wolsingham to Frosterley. Heading from Wolsingham it is the second parking space encountered. GR NZ 046 369.
MAP: OL31 North Pennines.
DOGS: With the route being all on public rights of way then dogs are allowed, however, as livestock will be encountered throughout this route please keep them under close control.. The route does pass through a number of farmyards and so it is very likely that you will encounter other dogs. Also a number of the stiles encountered on the walk are high, narrow and awkward stiles built into the stone walls and you may have to lift them over, If they are large dogs then this may be a 'fun' experience.
ACCESS: The route is all on public rights of way.

GRID REFERENCES:

Lay-by	046 369
Newlands Hall	046 375
Footbridge	049 386
Gate	055 392
Track/path junction	064 382
Path/road junction	068 378
Newlands Hall	046 375
Lay-by	046 369

FGS GRADING:
Grading is T5 [D0, N1, T1, R1,H2]

Distance	0	Up to 6 miles
Navigation	1	Basic navigation skills needed
Terrain	1	50 – 75% on graded track or path 25 – 50% off track
Remoteness	1	Countryside in fairly close proximity to habitation – at least 80% of the route within 2 miles
Height	2	Over 125 ft per mile

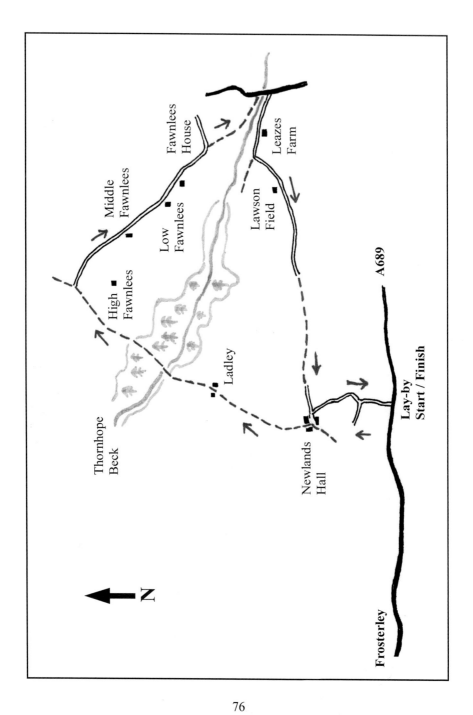

THE WALK

1. From the western end of the lay-by, cross the road and head up the tarmac drive to Newlands Hall and West Newlands Farm, see photo below.

The tarmac drive heading up to Newlands Hall and West Newlands Farm.

Follow the drive as it slowly climbs up the side of the valley to cross a cattle grid and then come to a junction. Ignore the left branch to West Newlands Farm and turn right to continue climbing. Shortly after the junction and as the track is bending to the left, what appears to be a hollow way leaves the left side of the track and heads up the hill. This hollow way may be the original route of the track as it headed up the hill, the surface being eroded below ground level through centuries of use. Continue up the modern track to come to a gate leading into the farmyard of Newlands Hall. **GR 046 375.**

The hollow way that was passed on the way up the track was probably one of the access routes into a hamlet that once stood on the site of Newlands Hall. The hamlet of Newland and Fowleys existed at some point during the Medieval period,

The old hollow way leaving the drive.

from 1066 to 1540. It is not known why it disappeared, it could be one of many reasons ranging from plague to the whim of the lord of the manor or even a combination of more than one of these. To the south west of the Hall lie a series of Medieval field banks, once part of the agricultural system that supported the hamlet.

2. Go through the gate and turn left to follow the yard between the buildings. As you come to the end of these buildings you'll see a small wooden gate with a waymarker sign on, just in front of you. Don't go through it but instead turn right to go between the two barns and come to a double gate. There is no waymarker sign on the gates but it is a right of way, so go through the gates and follow the wall on the right until you come to a gate in it. Go through the gate and, ignoring the track that goes straight ahead, bear left heading diagonally up the bank making for the right hand of the two gates that you can see on the skyline. Once there, go through and bear right over the top of the rise making for the stone wall in that direction to come to a stile in the wall. Note that the stile is difficult to see until you are more or less on top of it. Go over and make for another stile that is visible in the wall diagonally on the left, once over head between the, now visible, two buildings of Ladley making for the gate in the wall behind them.

Making for the two buildings of Ladley.

Pass through and continue straight ahead, walking downhill and making for the trees of Ladley Wood. Along the way you'll cross a small stream but eventually you'll come to a fence where you turn left to follow it as it heads downhill to come to a footbridge over the Thornhope Beck. **GR 049 386.** Ignore the two stiles on either side of the bridge, which are marked as private access anyway, and cross the bridge.

3. Once on the other side, follow the waymarker up the distinctive path that goes up the side of the hill in front.

Following the waymarker up the side of the hill.

After a short but steep pull up the bank you'll come to a firebreak that runs along the top and here turn to the right for a few metres to come to a track corner. Turn left onto the track and continue heading uphill. When the fence on the right turns a corner, turn right with it following the track as it now runs in-between the fence and a wall. At the end when you come to a wooden gate, don't go through it but instead go through the small metal gate in the wall on the left. From this gate a faint path can be followed, crossing the ruined wall in front and heading up the hill towards a gap in the gorse. The aim is to make for a corner in the wall that can be seen on top of the bank and here there is a gate complete with that rarity on this walk, a waymarker.

Once at the gate, if you look over to the left the mound of Fatherley Hill Currick can be clearly seen on the skyline. As discussed previously, it is thought that these mounds did not just act as funeral sites but also as territorial markers. The visibility of this prehistoric monument shows the impact that this mound would have had when newly built.

Go through the gate and then bear left going across the slope of the hill and

79

Fatherley Hill Currick on the skyline.

making for the left side of the band of trees that can be seen straight ahead. As you approach the trees you'll cross another ruined wall before coming to a wall, complete this time, and a gate that leads onto a track. **GR 055 392.**

4. Go through the gate and follow the track as it heads downhill through the trees.

Continuing the theme of the prehistoric settlement of the valley that was developed earlier in the book, there was a discovery in the area surrounding the track of two artefacts. The first being a Bronze Age flanged axe and the second being half of a mace head, both now being in the British Museum in London.

The buildings of High Fawnlees are visible at a short distance over to the right and 600 metres after leaving the gate you'll pass the farm of Middle Fawnlees on the right side of the track. As you follow the track down you'll pass a number of footpaths leaving off it but it is easy to stay on the obvious main track. Another 400 metres after passing Middle Fawnlees you'll pass Low Fawnlees.

Very nicely restored, Low Fawnlees is a 18th century farmhouse dating from the mid 1700's with some late 19th century additions. Built from coursed squared rubble and with a stone flagged roof, the house is a listed building.

Not long after this you'll then come to Fawnlees House.

Shown on the OS map as Fawnlees Hall, the building is now known as Fawnlees House. The original building was built in the late 1600's with later addi-

tions and alterations in 1787 and the early 1900's. The building is a grade 2 listed building along with a 18th century gazebo located in the gardens at the rear of the house.

A short distance after Fawnlees House, the track takes a sharp left hand turn (**GR 064 382**) and here leave it to cross the stile in front and go straight across the field making for the right hand of the two gates ahead of you where you will find a stile next to it. Once across the stile head to the wall on the left but go past the gate and follow the wall down to a corner where you pick up a distinctive path. Bear left to follow the path round the corner and descend towards a gate and a large ladder stile over the fence. Go through the gate, it has the waymarker on and is a lot easier to negotiate than the stile. Once through bear right across the field making for the visible bridge where you will find a stile leading onto the road. **GR 068 378.**

Thornhope Beck Bridge.

Built in the late 1700's Thornhope Beck Bridge has provided the crossing over the waters of the beck for almost three hundred years. Constructed from sandstone rubble in a single arch design, the bridge is now, itself, another listed building.

5. Turn right onto the road to cross over the bridge and a short distance after it, as shown by the footpath sign, turn right up the track for Leazes Farm. Continue up the track for 300 metres where it bears right to go round the farm. Shortly after this come to a point where the track turns sharply left and immediately in front of you is a waymarker. Ignore the waymarker and continue following the track round to the left and past the buildings of Lawson Field, shown on the OS map as Lason Field. Continue following the track as it becomes fenced on both sides and heads between a series of fields.

Following the track between the fields.

Eventually the track ends at a gate, go through and head straight across the open field to a stile in the stone wall opposite. Climb over and, once again, head straight over the open field but bearing slightly to the left making for a gate opposite. Go through and follow the edge of the field, keeping the hedge on your left, to come to another gate this time with a waymarker. Follow the rough track ahead keeping to the left of the fence, through two gates to arrive once again in the farmyard of Newlands House and, conveniently, at the top of the access drive. **GR 046 375.**

6. Turn left through the gate and follow the tarmac track back down the hill to the main road, the lay-by and the car.

Cowhorse Hush.
Walk 8. Cowhorse Hush & Cuthbert's Level.

WALK 8: COWHORSE HUSH & CUTHBERT'S LEVEL

At the top end of Weardale lies a relic of the old lead mining days. Nothing so small as a level entrance or the 'donut' of a shaft, this stretches a full three quarters of a mile down the side of the hill and is deep enough to hide three double-decker buses.

Cowhorse Hush is the biggest and deepest hush within Weardale and one of the largest in the North Pennines. A man-made excavation cut deep into the side of the hill, nearly three hundred years of toil and back-breaking labour forced a massive quantity of ore from the vein beneath this hill.

DISTANCE: 5.8 mile / 9.3 km
ASCENT: 833 feet / 254 metres
TERRAIN: The bulk of the walk is on field path and track. However, there are sections of the walk, at the top end of the valley, where you walk over open moor and rough pasture, both of which can be wet and uneven underfoot. There are two stream crossings, the Killhope Burn and the Wellhope Burn, where you have to cross without the aid of a bridge. In wet weather or times of high water then it may be advisable not to do this walk. There is a long steady climb over rough ground up the side of Cowhorse Hill and the descent down to the Wellhope Burn crossing can be a bit rocky and slippery.
TIME: 4½ to 5 hours.
START: Car park on the right of the main road as you enter Cowshill from the east. GR NY 857 406.
MAP: OL31 North Pennines.
DOGS: With the route being on public rights of way then dogs are allowed. However, you will find fences where they will need to be lifted over, farmyards where you will meet farm dogs, two streams to cross without the use of bridges, livestock, including ducks and geese, in very close proximity throughout the route plus when you are in the mining areas there will be holes in the ground where you will have to make sure that your dog doesn't enter. In short, even though they may be allowed it may be advisable not to take your dog on this walk.
ACCESS: The route is all on public rights of way apart from the two little 'explores' around Cowhorse Hush and Cuthbert's Level where you are utilising access land. However, the paths around Wellhope and Hole Dam are not well walked or marked and so you can find yourself easily straying off the public footpath.

GRID REFERENCES

Car park	857 406
Heathery Bridge	845 413
Road	836 422
Path/track junction	826 421
Cuthbert's Level	825 420
Hole Dam	830 412
Path/track junction	837 413
Heathery Bridge	845 413
Car park	857 406

FGS GRADING:

Grading is F5 [D0, N1, T1, R1,H2]

Distance	0	Up to 6 miles
Navigation	1	Basic navigation skills needed
Terrain	1	50 – 75% on graded track or path 25 – 50% off track
Remoteness	1	Countryside in fairly close proximity to habitation – at least 80% of the route within 2 miles
Height	2	Over 125 ft per mile

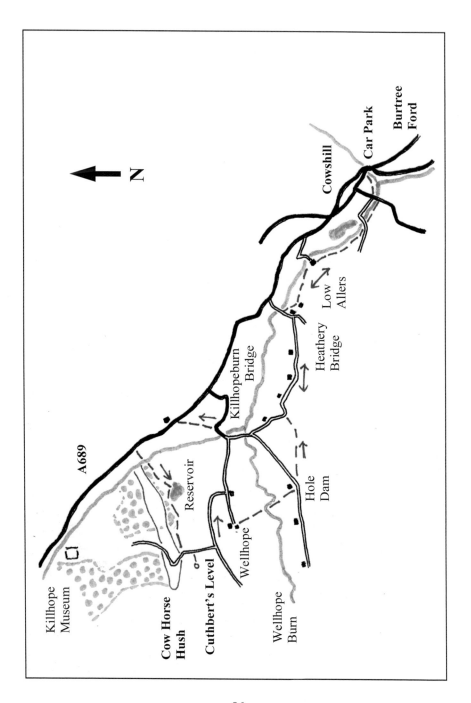

Killhope
Museum

A689

Cow Horse
Hush

Cuthbert's Level

Wellhope

Wellhope
Burn

Reservoir

Hole
Dam

Killhopeburn
Bridge

Heathery
Bridge

Low
Allers

Cowshill

Car Park

Burtree
Ford

N

THE WALK

1. From the car parking space go back to the main road and turn right to cross the footbridge over the Sedling Burn. When you are over, immediately turn left to cross the road to the footpath sign and stile opposite. Cross and descend down the path that runs high above the burn to come to a track at the bottom. Here turn right to go past " The Mill " and after a few hundred metres come to a roadside next to the Burtreeford Bridge.

Burtreeford Bridge.

Turn left to cross the bridge and a couple of metres up, on the right side of the road, leave at the footpath signpost and go down the bank and alongside the wall to the waymarked stile. Cross and follow the left bank of the Killhope Burn upstream. After a short distance you'll come to a footbridge crossing the burn. Don't cross the stile, instead stay on the left side of the fence and go through the gap between the wall and fence in front to come to a vehicle bridge.

The 'small, barely noticeable' flooded quarry on the other side of the bridge is Copthill Quarry. Producing whinstone from 1895 to 1943, this quarry is a stark reminder of the various mineral extraction industries and their effects on this valley. Now, filled with water and with nature slowly softening the edges it seems to fit this rugged landscape. A quick out and back visit over the bridge can give you a closer look.

Continue to follow the left bank of the Killhope Burn upstream. In a short while the path will leave the burn to cut across a field and approach the buildings of Low Allers. Go through the waymarked gate and continue straight ahead on the track between the buildings. When the main track bends to the left, continue straight ahead on the more minor track. At the end of the field the track turns sharply left to go up to a cottage and here leave it to go through a gap in the

The flooded Copthill Quarry.

wall on the right. Once through continue straight ahead, with the wall now on your left, for 30/40 metres to a kissing gate at the end of the field. Pass through and follow the path on the left side of the ruined wall, in-between the wall and the narrow stream. This will bring you to a large duck pond, normally quite full of geese and ducks so expect some noise, and go round the left side of the pond to a small gate in the wall at the other end. Once through the gate, you'll find a marker post that directs you down alongside the fence on the right towards the Heathery Bridge which is visible ahead. This short stretch is normally wet and

Following the fence down to the Heathery Bridge.

88

boggy in places but brings you down to the banks of the burn which you follow to the base of the bridge and then climb the steps up to it. **GR 845 413.**

2. Don't cross the bridge, instead turn left to follow the track up to the cottage and just after the cottage come to a junction. Bear right to follow the track past the big green chimney that is set in the field. Continue on the track past Middle Rush and when you get to the next farm, High Rush, the track goes through a gate to the left of the buildings and once past the buildings, turns right through a gateway before continuing straight ahead. After a short while, the track bends to the left before turning right again to descend down to pass Blakeley Field. Not long after passing these buildings you'll come to a junction and here bear right to cross the bridge over the Wellhope Burn. Next you'll come to another junction, this one with a footpath marker post, and here bear right again, to descend to Killhopeburn Bridge and the ruined building sat next to it.

Crossing the Killhopeburn Bridge.

Built during the 1800's to service the lead mines and farmsteads on the south side of the burn, this bridge is really two bridges with the older stone arched bridge alongside another stone bridge which contains three metal tubes through which the burn flows.

Here the track joins a narrow tarmac road, so follow the road and when you come to the corner where it bends right, cross the cattle grid and leave the road at the footpath marker post. A couple of metres after the signpost there is a bit of an old rough path leaving the side of the road which is slightly easier than leaving the road at the signpost itself. Follow this rough path up to the next signpost and then continue in the same direction going past an old quarry on the right. In places the path appears to be sunken, indicating an extensive usage over a long period of time, sufficient to wear the surface of the path below ground level. When you get over the rise, make for the house that you can see on the skyline and you'll come to a gate in the wall on the left. Go through and cross the corner of the field, going over a gully made by an old water channel on the way and make for a footpath signpost next to a gate that leads onto the road. **GR 836 422.**

3. Turn left to follow the road for 400 metres till you come to a footpath sign and stile on the left side of the road.

The Killhope Lead Mining Museum.

From this point the course of the upper valley can be seen straight ahead including the world famous Killhope Lead Mining Museum on the valley floor next to the burn. Unfortunately the large water wheel for which the museum is well known can't be seen for the side of one of the buildings. If you get the chance I can personally recommend a visit to Killhope including a trip into the old Park Level mine.

Cross the stile and head straight down towards the burn making for the left hand side of the wood. When you get to the valley floor you'll find the Killhope Burn

90

in one of it's most delightful moods as it runs along it's rocky bed, tumbling over a low waterfall. On the opposite bank a footpath marker can be seen on the fence. Cross the burn, which under normal conditions is quite easy, and then

Crossing the Killhope Burn.

clamber over the wooden part of the fence to follow the left side of the wood up the hill. After a short distance you'll have to clamber over another fence and not long after this you'll come to a water course cutting across your path. If you look to your left here, you'll see a footpath marker post, leave the boundary of the wood and follow the left side of the gully to the marker post and then onto the old Collierhill Reservoir.

At the reservoir turn right to follow the path along the bank back over to the side of the wood and continue following the wood's boundary up the hill. You'll soon come to a gateway in a fence which also marks the top of the wood on the right, the trees in front actually form part of a separate wood. Go through the gateway and less than a hundred metres away on the right lies a huge gash in the earth that is the Cowhorse Hush. The path follows the edge of the hush for a short distance to come to a newly-built vehicle track at **GR 826 421.** However, it is an easy enough descent down into the hush for a little exploring. Locating the new track afterwards is straight forward.

4. Once on the new track turn left irrespective of whether you join it at the top of the hush or where the path joins it. Dependant upon where you join the track you may see some footpath markers on the right side of it but ignore these to go past a small fenced off area also on the right. About 20 metres after passing the fence, the track goes over a small, narrow stream and there are some grassed over spoil heaps over on the right. Leave the track here for an out and back diversion to Cuthbert's Level. Turn right to follow the stream for 100 metres, going past the spoil heaps, to come to the level entrance out of which the stream flows. **GR 825 420.**

The course of the stream past the spoil heaps towards Cuthbert's Level and, inset, the level entrance.

5. Return back to the track and continue heading downhill to come to a junction. Turn left and follow the track through a gate and into an area of recently planted trees. The track bends to the right and descends out of the trees to come to a waymarked junction in front of a cottage. Ignore the signpost and turn right to head to the buildings of Wellhope. When you get there follow the track past the house on the right and go to the left of the small building, through the gate behind it and then immediately turn left to head for the gateway in the wall below. Go through the gateway and the path now heads straight down the field to come to a fence line. At the time of the test walking there was no way over this fence so turn left and follow the fence a couple of hundred metres to the field corner and go through the ramshackle gate that you'll find there. Be careful as you follow the small stream down to the

Wellhope Burn, the descent is a bit steep and slippery. Use the many stones to cross the main burn and once over, go straight ahead to a fence in front and then turn right to follow the fence to a gate next to the tell-tale donut of an old shaft. Go through the gate and then through the gap in the ruined wall on the other side of it, now head for the gate on the right side of the farm buildings in front and exit onto a track next to the farm of Hole Dam. **GR 830 412.**

6. Turn left to go across the farmyard and through the gate on the other side. Then as the track bends left, leave it to follow a set of muddy wheel prints forming a rough track going off from the right side of the main track. Follow this rough track across the field to come to a gate next to a line of old shafts. Once through the gate you'll find a number of faint tracks. Follow the one that bears left over towards the wall, ignore the two red gates and follow the outside of the wall around, keeping it on your left, for about 300 metres to come to a track. **GR 837 413.**

7. The track that you have just joined is the same one that you came out on and from here you are retracing your steps back to Cowshill. Turn right on to the track and follow it back up past the farms and then down to Heathery Bridge.

Descending down to the Heathery Bridge with the arches of the Heathery Cleugh Bridge in the background.

As you descend down to Heathery Bridge you get good views of the impressive Heathery Cleugh Bridge. Built around 1810 the five tall, slender arches of the bridge carry the main dales road over the deep valley of the Heathery Cleugh. With it's elegant structure it's not really surprising that the bridge is a listed building.

Here, again, don't cross the bridge, turn right down the steps to the side of the burn and then follow the waymarkers up the side of the hill to the gate next to the cottage. Once through the gate go round the top of the duck pond and follow the right side of the ruined wall to the next gate. Go through and from here follow the left side of the wall to the gap at the end of the field, here go through and onto the track to continue straight ahead down to Low Allers. As the track goes between the buildings and turns left, leave it to go through the waymarked gate in front and into the fields to follow the path to and along the side of the burn. After you have passed the bridge over to the old quarry and the footbridge, you'll come to the stile leading onto the road next to the Burtreeford Bridge. Go up to the road, turn left to cross the bridge and then turn immediately right to go down the lane between the houses. When you approach the bridge over the Sedling Burn, don't cross but turn left to go past the short row of cottages, up the steps at the end of them and onto the green path that runs high above the burn to emerge onto the main road in front of the Cowshill Hotel. Cross the road and turn right to go over the footbridge and then turn left into the car park.

COWHORSE HUSH

Cowhorse Hush is a great gash cut into the southern side of Weardale. Stretching for ¾ mile from near the top of Cowhorse Hill all the way down to the side of the Killhope Burn, this deep, wide excavation is the result of almost two hundred years of digging for lead. The lower section of the hush being hidden within the trees of the modern plantation.

Hushing is a method of mining that uses water to wash away the top soil and any loose rocks and stones to expose the lead vein. Indeed the name 'hush' is thought to come from the sound the water made when it rushed down through the workings.

Dams were made on the top of the hill to gather and build up a sufficient head, or volume, of water. Quite often a very sophisticated system of water channels, known as leats, was built to bring water into the reservoir created by the dam, in some cases from several miles away. When sufficient water was collected then it would be released by a sluice from the dam and directed down a particular route by laid out channels through the workings.

This rush of water would sweep away the topsoil, vegetation and loose rocks exposing the vein. Then the work would start with pick and shovel, loosening and working the ore from the ground which would continue for days or weeks

The reservoir of Collierhill Dam and, inset, the stone-lined sluice.

until another head of water had built up again behind the dam. Once more the water would be released and afterwards the men would return with pick and shovel. This process being repeated continuously over the years. Although water force was a major contributor to the excavation of a hush, it was the sheer strength of a miner's arms and back that created the bulk of it.

As with any hushes of great length, the power of the water is dispersed the further down the hush that it has to run. To counter this, dams and water channels were often built further down the hush so that the flow could be easier directed down to the lower workings. The Collierhill Dam, passed on the climb up the hill next to the plantation, is one such example. The leat which is followed on the climb up the hill, takes the water down and into the lower reaches of the hush hidden amongst the trees.

As it enters the wood, the depth of the middle section of the hush dwarfs the electricity poles that run across it.

Although environmentally damaging, working a hush can be a very effective method of extracting ore. However, there are limits as to how far down into the earth a hush can follow a vein. Ultimately the point is reached where a level, a horizontal tunnel driven into the side of the hill, is the only method of accessing those parts of the vein deep within the ground.

As part of the early exploitation of the vein, a level was driven in 1794 from Lingy Brow Spring into the upper reaches of the vein above the top of the hush.

Operated by a partnership of four miners working for the Beaumont Company, this was known as Cuthbert's Level.

As the output from the hush began to diminish during the 1850's, the Beaumont Company who were the owners of the mining lease, drove three levels at various heights into the hush to continue working the vein. Logically enough, these were called Cowhorse Low Level, Middle Level and Top Level. The Low Level was driven into the hill from the banks of the Killhope Burn, higher up the hill the Middle Level was driven and the Top Level went in near the top of the hush. It is the Top Level that is passed on this walk.

Using the hush and the levels, between 1847 and 1876 over 2,400 tons of ore were extracted. As the earliest known record of work on this vein is dated 1761 and it was very probably being worked before this, then the scale of the excavations suggest that this was only a small amount of the total volume of ore obtained from this vein. Working at the hush ended around 1880.

The workings at the top end of the hush with, inset, the Top Level entrance located on the left side of the hush a hundred metres or so in front of the track.

The old cutting leading to Fine Burn Quarry.

WALK 9: THE QUARRIES OF BOLLIHOPE

A lower level walk that roughly follows the course of the Bollihope Beck from it's mouth, where it joins the River Wear, to where it emerges onto the open moor.

In the past, the valley of the Bollihope Burn has been heavily exploited for it's mineral wealth with the landscape being cut and carved by the hand of man. The majority of these sites are no longer used and nature is in the slow process of

98

reclaiming them back as her own. This has, in itself, given rise to a new rich and varied landform, born of both man and nature.

Part of this walk follows the route of the Mineral Valley Walk set up by Durham County Council and along the way encounters a number of information boards that explain these sites, what you can see and the site's part in the industrial history of the valley.

DISTANCE: 6.2 miles / 9.9 km
ASCENT: 453 feet / 138 metres
TERRAIN: Mainly field paths and tracks.
TIME: 4 to 4½ hours.
START: Frosterley Station Car Park. GR NZ 024 369.
MAP: Explorer OL31 North Pennines.
DOGS: The route is all on rights of way and so dogs are allowed but keep them under close control. Livestock can be expected throughout the walk.
ACCESS: The route is all on public rights of way.

GRID REFERENCES:

Frosterley Station	024 369
Caravan park entrance	047 368
White Kirkley	027 360
Bottom of track	015 352
Track/path junction	017 353
Road	025 360
Frosterley Station	024 369

FGS GRADING:
Grading is T4 [D1, N1, T1, R1,H0]

Distance	1	6 – 12 miles
Navigation	1	Basic navigation skills needed
Terrain	1	50 – 75% on graded track or path 25 – 50% off track
Remoteness	1	Countryside in fairly close proximity to habitation – at least 80% of the route within 2 miles
Height	0	Less than 100 ft per mile

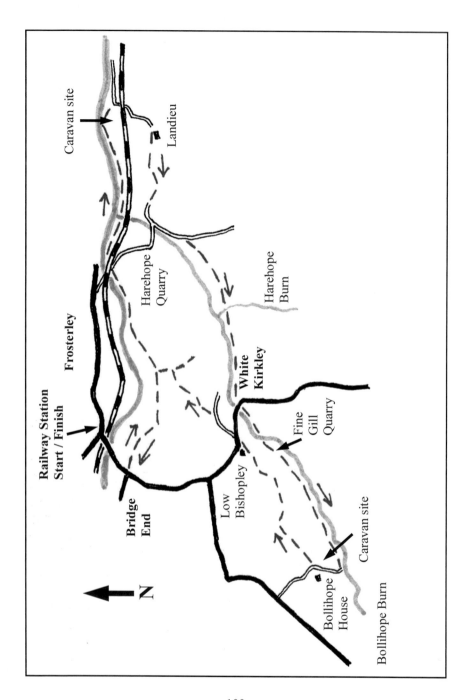

Caravan site

Landieu

Frosterley

Harehope
Quarry

Harehope
Burn

White
Kirkley

Railway Station
Start / Finish

Fine
Gill
Quarry

Bridge
End

Low
Bishopley

Caravan site

N

Bollihope
House

Bollihope Burn

THE WALK

1. Leave the station car park and turn left to follow the road across the bridge over the River Wear. Staying on the left, continue following the road up and into Bridge End until you come to a lane on the left next to the church.

The lane by the side of the church.

Turn left and follow the lane between the houses and this becomes a track leading to East Bridge End Farm. When the track turns right into the farm, continue straight on following the waymarked path. Continue on through a gate and when you come to a metal kissing gate, ignore the path leading off to the right to go through it. The path is now running along a bank high above the river but continue and shortly you'll pass a path on the left that heads down to the riverbank. As you have walked, you'll have passed the old workings of Broadwood Quarry on your right and now you'll start passing the yards and buildings. Stay on the path running to the left of these and keep next to the river. Once past the quarry you'll come to a level crossing that goes over the rail line of the Weardale Railway. Turn left to go over the crossing but before you cross the bridge over the Wear turn right to follow a path running between some allotments. Once past the allotments the path enters fields and starts to run along the left side of the rail line. Stay on the obvious, well-trodden path and you'll come to a footbridge over the Bollihope Burn.

The Bollihope Burn joining the River Wear.

The mouth of the burn, where it runs into the River Wear, is just a short distance away and, if you wish, it is easy enough to nip between the gorse bushes to see it.

Continue on the path as it runs between river and railway and eventually it moves away from the rail line to skirt round the outside of a caravan park. Towards the end of the caravans, the path turns right to enter and go through the caravan park, passing the reception buildings and exiting at the main entrance to the park. **GR 047 368.**

2. From the entrance you join the Weardale Way and follow it for the next 2 km to White Kirkley. So leave the park entrance and turn right to follow the farm track as it crosses the rail line and goes to the farm of Landieu. Once at the farm take the path straight ahead between the buildings, going through first the red gate and then the gate behind it. Go diagonally across the next field making for a gate in the far corner of the field. Pass through and then follow the wall on the right through the next field and half way down the length of the following field to come to yet another gate, this one giving access onto an enclosed track. Follow this track for a couple of hundred metres to come to a junction. The right hand turning crosses a bridge over the Bollihope Burn to give access to the Harehope Quarry Project but don't go that way. Instead bear to the left and follow the track for a further 100 metres before leaving it and going through a way-marked gate on the right and into a field. Once in the field, the path follows the field boundary on the right as it runs high above Harehope Quarry. As it does so, the full layout of this reclamation project is laid out below you.

Looking across to the Harehope Quarry.

When you've past the quarry, the path does a slight kink to the right in the last field to leave it half way down the far wall and enter a small area of woodland that lines the banks of the Harehope Gill.

Here find an information board on the Harehope Gill Lead Mine which was located in this small valley.

Cross the footbridge over Harehope Burn which runs down the gill and follow the fairly well-defined path as it makes it's way along the left bank of the Bollihope Burn, passing through several fields on the way.

As you walk along the burn you'll encounter an information board pointing out the Bishopley Lime Kilns which lie opposite the board.

The Bishopley Lime Kilns.

After 500 metres bear to the right of the building in front of you, to exit onto the road in White Kirkley. **GR 027 360.**

3. Turn right onto the road and follow it for the short distance down to the bridge over the Bollihope Burn but before crossing it, turn left at the footpath marker post to follow the left bank of the burn upstream. After 300 metres the path crosses a footbridge to now start following the burn's right bank. The path is very easy to follow as it sticks fairly close to the side of the burn deviating slightly every now and again. The path itself, passes through an old cutting between the rocks to enter the remains of the Fine Burn Quarry and, surprisingly enough, this steep-sided little valley of the Bollihope is very pleasant to walk up despite all the remains of the quarrying industry. Nature has spent years slowly reclaiming these sites and now they all seem to balance each other out in a very eye-pleasing harmony.

The path alongside the burn leading away from Fine Burn Quarry.

The path is followed up the valley, going past a second footbridge, as it makes it's way, until the woods suddenly give way to an open landscape. Shortly after this an old cottage, which is now a holiday home, is passed and then you come to the bottom end of a track complete with waymarker. **GR 015 352.**

The old cottage alongside the Bollihope Burn.

4. Turn right to follow both the direction shown by the waymarker and the track as it goes uphill into the caravan site that is situated above you. As you pass through the site, you'll come to a junction where you bear left to come to the buildings of Bollihope House, which is the reception building of the site. As you become level with the buildings a footpath sign on the right shows you the route away from the track and across the fields. **GR 017 353.**

5. Leave the track and head across the field following the direction of the footpath sign to come to a wall and then, keeping the wall on your left, follow it across the field to enter a second field. Again start following the wall on the left and when that turns away, head across the field making for the corner where a wall and fence meet. Once at the corner, follow the fence to come to a gate that leads onto a track. Pass through the gate and follow the track as it makes it's way through the fields to eventually come out between the buildings of Low Bishopley Farm and onto the road. **GR 025 360.**

6. Opposite the entrance to the farm but slightly to the left, stands a footpath post next to a gate. Cross the road and, following the directions of the footpath sign, go through the gate and follow the track down the slight descent. When you get to the bottom there are several other tracks and there is also, quite handily, a waymarker post that shows the way, the track that you want bears left up a steep bank.

The bottom of the track where you head up the bank.

At the top of the bank cross into the next field and then follow the field boundary on the left round to the end of that field. Here turn left into the next field and follow the fence downhill going past an old quarry to come to a metal kissing gate. Don't go through the gate which, incidentally is the one that you encountered on the way out from Bridge End, but instead turn left and follow the path and it's waymarkers past East Bridge End Farm to ultimately join the road at Bridge End. Once back at the road turn right to retrace your steps across the bridge over the River Wear and back to Frosterley Station.

APPENDIX

Ferguson Grading System (`FGS`)

1. Introduction

The FGS has been adopted as a means of assessing the nature and severity of the various walks in this book and the abilities and equipment needed to tackle each one safely. The FGS was developed by Stuart Ferguson, a long time fell and trail runner, climber, mountaineer, mountain-biker and general outdoor enthusiast. In the opinion of Trailguides, the FGS is the most accurate and comprehensive grading system for comparing off-road walking, running and mountainbiking routes anywhere in the country.

2. The System

Tables 1 & 2, set out below, are used in order to give a grading to each route. Table 1 sets out three categories of country that a route could potentially cross, together with a range of factors that would need to be considered when tackling that route. The three categories are, Trail, Fell and Mountain, and after assessing which category best fits the route, a letter, either `T`, `F` or `M`, is allocated to that route. Where a route does not fit perfectly into one of the three categories the closest category is allocated.

Table 2 deals with five specific aspects of the route, distance, navigation, terrain, remoteness and height gain, and each one is allocated a letter, `D`, `N`, `T`, `R`, and `H`. Each letter is also given a severity score from the range 0-3 or 0-4, in respect of distance (`D`). The higher the number, the more severe the route. The five severity scores are then added together to give an overall score. The overall score is then put with the Table 1 category letter (i.e. `T`, `F` or `M`).

In order to show how the grading has been determined for each walk in this book, the five individual severity scores are set out, in square brackets, immediately after the actual grading. So, for example, Walk 1 Fatherley Hill & Wolsingham Park Moor has a grading of F7 [D1, N1, T1, R2, H2], indicating that it is a Fell Category walk with a total severity score of 7. This is made up of the five specific severity scores, for distance (`D`), navigation (`N`), terrain (`T`), remoteness (`R`) and height gain (`H`), of 1, 1, 1, 2 and 2 respectively. The highest total severity score which can be achieved is 16 and the lowest total severity score achievable is 0.

The table which accompanies the grading for each walk sets out the specific factors, extracted from Table 2, that need to be considered when tackling that particular walk.

107

TABLE 1

	TRAIL	FELL	MOUNTAIN
Description	Lowland and forest areas including urban, cultivated and forested locations.	Moorlands and upland areas which may include some upland cultivated and forestry areas plus possibly remote locations.	Upland and mountain areas including remote and isolated locations.
Height	Not usually above 1,000 feet but may go up to 2,500 feet	Usually above 1,000 feet, up to 2,500 feet and above.	Usually above 2,500 feet and up to 4,000 feet.
Way-marking	Usually	Limited	None
Terrain	Usually graded paths, tracks and trails but may include some off-trail	May include some graded paths, tracks and trails but mainly off-trail	Virtually all off-trail
Height gain	Limited height gain	May include considerable height gain	May include some severe height gain.
Effects of weather	Very limited effect	May be prone to sudden weather changes	Extreme weather a possibility
Navigational skills	None to basic	Basic to competent	Competent to expert
Equipment	Walking shoes/boots. Possibly waterproofs Food and drink dependant upon route.	3/4 season walking boots. Full waterproof cover. Possibly map and compass dependant upon route. Food and drink dependant upon route.	Mountain boots. Full waterproof cover. Map and compass. Food and drink
Escape Routes	Yes	Some	Some to nil

TABLE 2

Score	0	1	2	3	4
Distance	Up to 6 miles	6 – 12 miles	12 – 18 miles	18 miles +	24 miles +
Navigation	No navigation skills needed	Basic navigation skills needed	Competent navigation skills needed	Expert navigation skills needed	
Terrain	75% + on graded track or path	50 – 75% on graded track or path / 25 – 50% off track	25 -50% on graded track or path / 50 – 75% off track	Under 25% on graded track or path / Over 75% off track	
Remoteness	Urban	Countryside in fairly close proximity to habitation – at least 80% of the route within 2 miles	Countryside not in close proximity to habitation – less than 20% of the route within 2 miles	Remote, isolated location	
Height gain	Less than 100 ft per mile	Over 100 ft per mile	Over 125 ft per mile	Over 250 ft per mile	

Notes to Table 2

Graded paths = Well established paths with a stable surface.

Escape routes = The opportunity to cut the route short and return to the start without completing the full course in the event of weather changes or unforeseen incidents.

The Author

Keven Shevels

Kev has been involved with outdoor sports for over forty years since his school days doing the Duke of Edinburgh award, spending his time either walking, running and latterly mountain biking through the countryside of the North East and beyond. He is not ashamed to admit that he is one of these boring people who can sit and spend hours reading a map the way that other people read a book.

His great delight is coming up with new routes that he can subsequently explore and investigate especially if he can couple this with his interest in history, in particular the prehistoric. This usually means much more than a walk as his routes tend to take a view not only on the landscape but also its relationship with events and occurrences that have happened in the past. In many ways this curiosity and knowledge of the Durham Dales can make him a perfect guide to this under-valued part of our region.

Now in his fifties, Kev has been unable to continue his running due to injury problems but instead has been co-author of one of the most innovative series of coaching books for fell and trail runners in recent years. He now brings his easy to read, informative style of writing to guide books for those who walk in the countryside of County Durham, his home county.

The author having a break out in the Durham countryside.

110

Walking North East

Walking North East is the brand name for the walking publications produced by Trailguides and reflects the pride that we, as North Easterners, have in our countryside, our history and our culture.

Based in Darlington, we are a small independent publisher specialising in guidebooks centred on the North Eastern counties of England. Our target is to produce guides that are as user-friendly, easy to use and provide as much information as possible and all in an easily readable format. In essence to increase the enjoyment of the user and to showcase the very best of the great North Eastern countryside. Our series of books explores the heritage of us all and lets you see your region with new eyes, these books are written to not just take you on a walk but to investigate, explore and understand the objects, places and history that has shaped not just the countryside but also the people of this corner of England.

If you've enjoyed following the routes in this guide and want news and details of other publications that are being developed under the Walking North East label then look at the company website at **www.trailguides.co.uk**

Comments and, yes, criticisms, are always welcomed especially if you discover a change to a route. Contact us by email through the website or by post at Trailguides Limited, 35 Carmel Road South, Darlington, Co Durham DL3 8DQ.

Other walking books from Walking North East.
At the time of publication the following books are also available but with new titles being regularly added to our publication list keep checking our website. All of these publications can be purchased as books or downloads from our website.

Northumberland.
The Cheviot Hills.
Walks from Wooler.
The Hills of Upper Coquetdale.
Walks from Kirknewton.
Walks on the Wild Side: The Cheviot Hills.
Walks Around Rothbury and Coquetdale.

County Durham.
Hamsterley Forest.
The Barningham Trail.
Ancient Stones.

The High Hills of Teesdale.
Walks from Stanhope.
Mid-Teesdale Walks.
Walking in Weardale.

North Yorkshire.
The Hills of Upper Swaledale.
Walks Around Gunnerside.
Walks around Reeth and Upper Swaledale.

Walking North East.
Visit our website and sign up to receive our free newsletter, Walking North East, dedicated to walking in North Eastern England. Full of news, views and articles relating to this the forgotten corner of England

Acknowledgements.
Are due to Harry Manuel for accompanying me on these walks and for being a fundamental part of the route testing procedure while occasionally appearing as the "model" in some of the photographs. Thanks are also due to my wife Lyn for the patience and tolerance shown while I "disappear" to walk and write about these routes.

Disclaimer
The information contained in these pages and the route descriptions is provided in good faith, but no warranty is made for its accuracy. The contents are, at the time of writing and to the best of our knowledge, up-to-date and correct. However, the world is a changing environment and what is correct one day may not be so the next. Care should always be taken when following these route descriptions just as it should when following maps or waymarkers of any kind..

No guarantee whatsoever is provided by the author and/or Trailguides Limited and no liability is accepted for any loss, damage or injury of any kind resulting from the use of this book, nor as a result of any defect or inaccuracy in it.

As with all outdoor activities, you and you alone are responsible for your safety and well being.